John Wayne and the Fierce Kuga-Kugas:
A Book of Healing and Transformation

Harvey R. Wasserman, MD

First published by Dog Ear Publishing
4010 W. 86th Street, Ste H
Indianapolis, IN 46268
www.dogearpublishing.net

ISBN: 978-1-4575-1288-9

This book is printed on acid-free paper.

Printed in the United States of America

CONTENTS

CHAPTER NINE – SPIRITUALITY AND MYSTICISM

CHAPTER TEN – INDEPENDENCE, LEARNING, MAKING MISTAKES

CHAPTER ELEVEN – THE HUMAN HEART

CHAPTER TWELVE – MAMA

CHAPTER THIRTEEN – SEARCHING FOR A FATHER

CHAPTER FOURTEEN – DOCTORING

Harvey R. Wasserman

INTRODUCTIONS

Introduction
Romeo In Winter

Introduction

THIS IS A BOOK about transformation both for me as writer and for you as reader.

Most "self-help" books make people feel better, perhaps give them some new ideas, but little or nothing changes. The result is more and more self-help books are written.

I want you to enjoy reading this book. Some of my stories are just for fun. I believe the right kind of laughter opens the brain to neuroplasticity (change in brain structure and content). Some of the fun stories had an essence that changed and expanded me. Perhaps they will do the same for you. If not, relax, don't worry.

Some points will be made explicit.

All my exercises are life changing. Try them if they appeal to you. See if they work for you. They need to be repeated for at least six weeks for the best neuroplastic result. Did you get a good response and only continue for a few repeats?

I hope my writing style in itself alters your state of consciousness. Reading a bit and then needing a break before continuing is a possible sign that this is taking place.

It is my fondest hope that finishing this book you will feel changed, that your life journey has been nudged forward and you won't know or necessarily care why.

If your significant other notices this transition before you do I would consider that a good sign.

One of my favourite patient results was with a psychologist who announced on terminating his work with me, "I have been promoted at work, and am getting great respect. I'm happier, my private practice has taken off; patients are not leaving. My wife and I are getting along, enjoying each other with all the benefits that that brings. My whole life has changed. I don't have a clue how you did it".

A positive result, but he will probably never become a student of mine.

NOTE: All stories, even the most unusual, are completely true.

Romeo In Winter, by Sarah Daniel

SIX AM, DECEMBER, a cottage in the West of Ireland. Middle of the week.

It is very dark.

The alarm clock screams. Harvey jumps out of bed to silence it. I cower under the duvet.

He opens the bathroom door, flips the switch, emits a wail of anguish at the blast of light assaulting him.

"Ahhhhhhhhh!" he protests. "Ahhhhhh! Ahhhhh! ...

> *Ah Juliet, 'tis the sun.*
>
> *Never thought we'd see another one.*
>
> *We feigned our death this day.*
>
> *We fooled them all and ran away.*"

I grab a pen and get it recorded.

Birth of a poem.

CHAPTER ONE

FEAR OF SUCCESS

John Wayne (Fame!)

THE STONE AGE was still alive in New Guinea in 1971.

Keith, an ex Australian Government patrol officer no longer employed to stop cannibalism and head hunting, was to guide me to a village twenty miles deep into the mountainous jungle. I wanted to hear their myths of origin and creation. He knew the chieftains, their language and all their customs.

We drove down a jungle trail in an open jeep.

At the outskirts of the village Keith shouted, "We are driving through!"

The natives had covered their skin with yellow clay. Some females had chopped off the ends of their fifth finger.

"They are very dangerous. Someone important has died. There is no belief in natural death. All deaths are murders or witchcraft. Discovery and justice must take place. Justice can vary from the killer giving a pig to the deceased family to killing someone in another village."

We drove through the village and had several interesting experiences that day.

The jungle trail home went right through the village. Anxious, we did not want to stop. But the chief was on the road and waved us down. It would have been an insult not to stop.

The chief came close to me as I cautiously left the jeep. He looked up at me and announced, "You John Wayne."

Puzzled, I looked to Keith. Keith nodded his head slowly, meaning "Yes, you're John Wayne."

A cry went up, "John Wayne!" Villagers crowded around me, touching John Wayne.

At first only the important people were allowed to get close. When introduced, I arrogantly pushed out my chest, shook hands and shouted, "Apinoon Pilgrim!" or "Apinoon Pardner!" (Apinoon means afternoon.) What excitement.

Keith asked my wife to take Polaroids of me with the important people (good PR). As she did, they asked, "Mary belong you?" ("Is that your woman?") Everyone wanted to touch my wife. She freaked while snapping the pictures.

I had three distinct reactions:

I had never been famous. It felt glorious to be so valued and admired.

I am not John Wayne, I am a phoney.

They will find out I am not John Wayne, and they will kill me.

After thirty-five to fifty minutes of jungle surrealism, Keith indicated we should leave.

"Keith, I was terrified that they would discover I was not John Wayne and would kill me."

"Not to worry. If John Wayne comes and claims to be John Wayne they will kill him."

They knew about John Wayne because the Australian government introduced the West by bringing in cowboy and Indian movies to the villages. Shooting, chasing, bows and arrows they understood.

They were encouraged to grow a little coffee for money. An enterprising Chinese man built a Quonset hut movie theatre in Mount Hagen and exclusively showed Westerns. They would walk forty miles to see their favourite, John Wayne.

I was Big John to everyone from then on.

I began to wonder why I had so carefully avoided becoming famous. Fame is a tool to make your dreams happen, just like political power or money. I love to be successful in making my dreams happen! So what was wrong?

Harvey R. Wasserman

Fear Of Success

ARE YOU AFRAID of success?

Did you answer no? The fear of success is in almost everyone. People are aware of their fear of failure. Hidden out of awareness is the fear of success. It is easy to know your desires and your fear of failure. It is difficult to know your fear of success. Any negative motivating force that is hidden has great power.

Look around you. FEAR OF SUCCESS IS OBVIOUS IN OTHERS, NOT IN OURSELVES.

I was trained to be a workaholic. Only hard work was admirable. The freedom of wealth isn't born that way. I can't get myself interested in investing! I am happy when I am creative or spiritual but have trouble staying with or starting my creative or spiritual self. I love the creative child in me and I fear him. I can always work hard.

A brilliant friend of mine, Bill, is well-positioned in corporate life. It so bores him that he hates going to work. He needs to run his own show. He manages to go into great debt by betting on and racing thoroughbred horses. When he is in deep debt, he focuses on a good short-term computer investment or winning bets at the track. He has been known to win $60,000 in one day and lose $20,000 the next and to walk into a bank with $80,000 in a shopping bag to pay off a loan. His family believes that success will destroy them; they never mention his corporate position and only respond to occasional wins at the track. He is caught in the energy of loss, then bailing yourself out. Talking to him, he listens, even agrees. Nothing changes. He needs to accumulate enough capital to start his own company that he could run at his own brilliant pace. He makes sure that this never happens.

Tom desperately wants to be a writer. A publisher was interested but wanted some re-writing. He procrastinated. There was no re-writing.

Mary was winning a ping-pong tournament. She found herself, as though in a trance, destroying the crucial final game.

Take responsibility for your failures. Have you contributed to them? Do you start things and not finish? Do you procrastinate (always fear-based) and lose the moment? Have you consistently made wrong decisions?

I was called to consult a woman who had married five men in a row who proved to be alcoholic, stole her money, and left.

An executive of a major multi-national corporation was found under his bed quaking with fear. His wife made an appointment for him. A powerful man strolled into my office. He always wanted to disprove his father's curse, "You will never be as successful as I am." He wanted to prove his father wrong. He needed a superior to tell him how wonderful he was. When the vice president sabotaged his reputation with the CEO, he was fired. It was the first failure he'd ever had. He ended up under his bed. Offers later came in to be a CEO of his own company or to work as an executive in another, smaller multi-national. Guess which one he took? He was too afraid to take the CEO offer and felt like a complete failure.

Awareness may come through a series of exercises.

Make contact with your eyes in a mirror. Verbalise the following sentences with a brief pause between each sentence. Notice if there is any alerting response in your mind or body:

1. "You are not afraid of success."

2. "You are afraid of success."

3. "As hard as it is for you to believe, you are afraid of success."

Now try a series of similar exercises with other parts of your life – love, career, money, adventure, excitement.

Ask yourself if the important people in your life were (are) constantly critical: "You're nobody; you will never become anything." Did they ignore you or, even worse, dislike you?

What wonderful things have people accused you of? Do you feel anxious and uncomfortable when this happens? The fear of success breeds low self-esteem. A useful exercise is don't cringe or apologise or deny. Train yourself to quickly say, "Thank you."

There are many imprinted beliefs that produce success fear. If I am successful, I will be killed, I will be abandoned, I will be leaned on, no one will take care of me. If I am successful, I will lose it. Only bad, immoral people are successful. I am just unsuccessful; that's who I am, I have to accept it. If I don't try, I haven't failed.

Success brings change and possibilities that can be scary. The parts of you that have to be faced and eliminated will disintegrate, and a replacement may take a while to appear. You may even feel like "I won't know who I am" for a while. Can you imagine other dangers?

Parents, for many reasons, may not love a child. Parents may be afraid of children outshining them. (Davy Crocket stopped killing bears one short of his father's record.) Parents sometimes fear being alone. They then want their children weak and dependent.

Happiness and success are twins and are vulnerable to similar supports and similar destructive influences.

Sit quietly and notice where in your head and body thoughts originate. Place your positive, successful thoughts in that place where thoughts seem to originate. I call this the centre of consciousness. You deserve all the good things in life. Do this regularly for at least six weeks. It's often not easy or pleasant to move through the prohibitions to success. So what? Whoever promised you it was going to be easy? No one is picking on you.

Remember Nelson Mandela's speech on his inauguration when he said, "Our deepest fear is not that we are inadequate, our deepest fear is that we are powerful beyond measure. It is our light, not our darkness that frightens us. We ask ourselves – who am I to be brilliant, gorgeous, talented and fabulous? You are a child of God. Your playing small doesn't serve the world, there is nothing enlightened about shrinking so that other people won't feel insecure around you. We were born to make manifest the glory of God that is within us. It is not just in some of us, it is in everyone. And as we let our light shine we unconsciously give other people's permission to do the same. As we are liberated from our own fear, our presence automatically liberates others."

For additional helpful ideas, take a peek at *Temporal Tapping* in Chapter 18.

Suppressing Einstein

FLUNKING ENGINEERING PHYSICS was a popular sport at Queens College.

I was working hard and barely getting a C. Final exam time, 9 am. I had read the schedule wrong. It was 1 pm. I had no books and was too far from home. I couldn't study.

Then I met super competitive Brian. He was hanging around school and challenged me to a three-and-a-half-hour game of killer ping-pong. Then on to engineering physics, two-and-a-half hours of serious testing.

I finished the test in twenty-five minutes. What was wrong? Everything was easy, like two and two is four. Confused, I asked for a pee break. I did not need to pee. I needed to make sense out of this unexplainable experience. No help. Back in the testing room, I reviewed everything. It only took me fifteen minutes. Everything was even simpler the second time around. I handed in my paper. Everyone else was seriously concentrating.

I got the only B in the course. I must have scored a perfect test paper. What happened? Did all that exercise push away the voices of self-constriction in my brain? What the hell. I forgot the whole thing.

Eight years later, my second-year supervisor at the Menninger Foundation School of Psychiatry assaulted me with, "Harvey, we are very dissatisfied with your performance here."

"What! I am one of the top three in my class."

"It doesn't mean shit. You scored so high on the admission test we gave you, your performance doesn't match up."

That night, although experienced with electric drills, I drilled through a piece of wood into my thigh and fainted!

I decided they must have gotten my test results confused with someone else. I knew how to penetrate the locked files to prove my hypothesis. I never did it. Can you guess why? I was afraid the file was true. That would have made it harder to forget the whole episode. Stay in everyday self-deluded normality.

At least it helped me understand patients who thought they were dull or simply average. They had been thoroughly convinced by somebody, mother or father, that they would never amount to anything and that they really were not too bright. They rejected the IQ tests I had them take which showed they were very bright. They assumed the results were falsified to make them feel better!

Top Amazon Warrior

IN THE 1970s, IQUITOS was a backward town in the upper Amazon area of Peru. Iquitos boomed in the early 1900s until the demand for rubber evaporated.

I engaged a Chinese gentleman to bring my wife and myself to visit an interesting tribal group located up one of the Amazon tributaries near Iquitos.

I have never before or since met a happier people. Their round, smiling faces brought peace and joy to the heart. Life was simple and easy, fish in the river, fruit on the trees, curare-laden blow guns, and bows and arrows if monkey protein was needed. They lived in one elongated log building elevated on tree stumps to keep snakes and moisture at bay. Much of their day was spent in socialising, singing, dancing and laughing. The women gathered around my wife and lifted her blouse. They had never seen breasts in a brassiere before. They pointed and laughed and brought all the females in the village to see this amazing sight.

The chief was carrying his bow and arrows, so what could I do but challenge him to an archery contest? Target – a large fruit in a tree about one hundred and fifty feet away. I am not very skilled with bows and arrows. His equipment was very different than the one I purchased from a sporting goods shop.

I was happy, content and at one with the universe as I drew my bow and sent the arrow to fruit dead centre.

The chief's turn – he missed! He did this for a living, my interest was just a hobby.

I ended the contest then and there.

Why? I knew I could never hit the target twice. I was no longer one with the equipment and the universe. I was one with my performance anxiety.

I learned that when there are no contaminating inner voices, we can all do amazing things. With the contaminating inner voices, no arrow flies straight.

The Greatest Warrior In New Guinea?

THEY WANTED to confiscate my bow and arrow at customs in New Guinea.

"What?" Most of the population are running around with bows and arrows. Tribal warfare is still very popular. I persisted, and they backed down. I had learned that bow and arrow shooting with the tribal chief in the Amazon produced a welcome response.

New Guinea has five hundred languages from five hundred tribal groups. Every tribe I spent time with, I organised a bow and arrow contest. They loved it. It was a new kind of entertainment and celebration. Some groups dressed up in their paint and feathers.

I always won. The mud men, with whom I had my first bow and arrow contest, were particularly rewarding. The women gathered around my wife and told her, "Your man great warrior." Since I always won, I offered a prize to whoever came in second best.

I am not a Robin Hood. They never developed feathers on their arrows. If I set the target at the right distance, I could hit it. At that distance, they couldn't hit the side of a barn. Without feathers, their arrows didn't fly true at a distance.

I was admired and accepted in each village. My prize of candy was appreciated, as sweets are very rare in the jungle.

I tried to teach some tribal groups about feathers. They were totally uninterested. They had been doing it their way for ten thousand years and saw no reason to change.

Harvey R. Wasserman

Fear Has No Place In Our Lives

THE GOOD NEWS is that there is nothing to be afraid of.

The bad news is that controlling fear, moving through fear, and eliminating fear, are not simple or easy tasks. Decreasing the control that fear has in your life by only 10 percent improves the quality of your life 100 percent. Here are four steps toward eliminating fear from your life:

Step 1: *Admit that you are afraid.* Many people bury their fears, yet when you are unaware of your fear, it can have massive, powerful control over your life.

Step 2: *Don't be judgmental about your fear.* You need to accept it as part of your existence, as something you have to learn to deal with more effectively or to eliminate. No one wants to be afraid. We all come by our fear naturally. If you beat yourself up, if you have contempt for yourself because you are afraid, your energy goes into traumatizing yourself, not into facing this fundamental life concern.

Step 3: *Make a heartfelt decision that you will not allow fear to control your life.* You will not allow fear to make the decisions that direct your existence. The courage to face your fears comes from *fear wisdom*. This is the belief that **not** facing fear is **more** dangerous than moving forward in the face of this unpleasant emotion.

Step 4: *Do anything you can to eliminate the fear that is within you.* No one gets through this life without fear. We all have to face fear if we are going to improve the quality of our existence.

It is very easy to drown your fear in alcohol. The unpleasant sensation goes away, but the fear goes into hiding, where fear has awesome power.

As children, we are born without the ability to take care of ourselves or to understand what our world is all about. Negative experiences, traumatic experiences, lay down fear pathways in the evolving brain that are much like ruts left by wagon wheels on a muddy road. These pathways have no sense of time. What might have made some sense to be afraid of as a child, no longer makes sense as an adult. But our minds react as if the fear was valid in present time. This timelessness of fear gives it great power.

Fear is necessary for children, *but it is totally unnecessary in adult life*. Children don't have judgment, knowledge or power. We as humans have such a long period of dependency and help-lessness in learning about the world around us that there is much time for trauma and false learning to engrave a deep sense of fear.

Imagine that there was a beam of wood on the floor of your living room and I ask you to walk across the living room bal-anced on that beam of wood. You are very likely to be able to do this. Now imagine the beam was suspended in the air over the Grand Canyon and I ask you to walk across it. You would prob-ably fall off. Did your fear help you to survive? It did not. Fear in the face of danger very often decreases the flexibility and speed of your ability to protect yourself. The Inuit (Eskimos) in their traditional culture learn to laugh in situations where we would feel afraid. Their environment is an extremely dangerous one.

Fear is one of the main culprits in human suffering and dys-function. The more you allow fear to run your life, the lower your self-esteem will sink. The more you face your fear, the more you eliminate fears, the more self-esteem you enjoy. Decrease fear and your independence increases: your creativity and energy increase. Fritz Perls, the developer of Gestalt psy-chotherapy, defines fear as your life force, your life energy, that has gotten constricted by future fantasies of disaster.

What are we afraid of? We are afraid of loss, of death. We also fear abandonment, embarrassment, shame and humilia-tion. These are the little deaths, the little murders. Fear is meant for survival of children. For an adult, it is useless. *There is nothing to be afraid of.* There are certainly dangers to be dealt with. That's different. Dealing is not fearing.

What can we do about this gremlin of fear? Moving forward in the face of fear is certainly useful, but often it will not make the fear go away.

Exercise is extremely helpful. Thirty-five minutes of aerobic exercise four or five times a week will almost immediately drop your levels of fear and anxiety. Aerobic simply means huffing and puffing.

Meditation has been known for thousands of years to decrease anxiety and fear. I have developed a form of meditation that is effective and simple. Instead of trying to control your thoughts, you allow your thoughts to do whatever they will. Sit in a relaxed and comfortable position. Attempt not to move and attempt not to swallow (you don't want to do this after eating). Attempting not to swallow sounds rather strange, but with a little practice, it's easy and comfortable to do. This is not an exercise in perfection, so no self-criticism. If you move or swallow, simply try not to move or swallow. Take 10 minutes now, attempt not to move and not to swallow. If you feel relaxed, increase meditation to 10-20 minutes twice daily.

Breath work is also helpful. (See the next section, *Breath Series*.)

Sometimes patients stop these exercises before they are healed, yet knowing that they help. Why? From fear of all the possibilities that are now available, and from the fear of moving away from a familiar though troubled lifestyle. That's how fearful we can be.

Breath Series

BREATH OF FIRE. All this means is that you breathe in and out as deeply and as fast as you can, through the nose. For most people, starting out with 6 or 8 is all they can do. The object is to build up to where you are doing about a minute and a half of such breaths.

There are four other steps in this exercise. In these exercises, breathe in through your nose and out through your mouth.

BEING BREATHED. Imagine for a couple of minutes, or longer if it suits you, not that you are breathing but that an outside benevolent force is 'breathing you.'

4-7-9 BREATHING. Take in a deep, vigorous inhalation through your nose. At the beginning of the inhalation, start a count from one to four, four being at the depth of that inhalation. At the end of the inhalation, hold your breath to the count of 7, at the same cadence as the inhalation. Blow out the breath through your mouth at the same cadence, to the count of 9.

With most people, I hope they can do 6 or 8 at the beginning and build up to a minute and a half or two minutes.

BREATH VISUALISATION. Just imagine you can see the breath about to enter your nostrils, going through your nostrils, down your throat, down your trachea, and inflating your lungs. Then reversing, moving out of your lungs, up your trachea, out your throat, and finally out of your mouth.

BREATH REVERSAL. (Sounds strange but is very helpful.) On inhaling through your nostrils, tell yourself that that is the end of breath, and when breathing out through your mouth, tell yourself that is the beginning of breath. Do this for one-and-a-half or two minutes.

Practice the Breath Series one or two times a day. If you practice it before meditation, your meditation may be enhanced.

Harvey R. Wasserman

The Rossi Technique

ERNEST ROSSI, a student of Milton Erickson, teaches a deceptively simple technique to help with any problem.

Hold your hands palm up, away from your body. In one hand place the problem. Permit the other hand to create whatever will help. Never relax the muscle tension on the arms. Allow the arms to move at their will.

That's it. You will know when you're done.

CHAPTER TWO

DESIRE, COMMITMENT, AWARENESS

Desire, Commitment, Awareness

EVERYONE WANTS SUCCESS, happiness, enough wealth, health, love, but often we don't get them. Why? Let us look at commitment. Commitment. What a remarkable word. What a remarkable idea. With it, almost anything can happen. Without commitment, little can happen.

If I have a patient committed to growth and healing, I can be a brilliant therapist. If I have a patient who is not committed to growth and healing, I am a therapist of limited ability. Little progresses or changes; or if it does, it is only temporary. I can tell the instant a patient achieves commitment to change some aspect of their life. It is as if a powerful engine suddenly comes to life, a powerful diesel motor in the bowels of a great ship. My interventions now work, fine-tuning the patient's committed energy for change.

What is this phenomenon called commitment? I think of it as a release of energy. Being 99% committed is like being 99% pregnant. It doesn't exist. What creates this wonderful state in which everything is possible, without which nothing is possible? Simple desire is not enough. Almost everyone desires the good things of life, but without the secret ingredient commitment they don't have any. Desire only releases power when there are no inhibiting internal beliefs, thoughts, attitudes or values, such as you can't, you shouldn't, it is dangerous, it is selfish. Desire supported with commitment is incredibly powerful. People often want to help you or at least get out of your way. Obstacles are not insurmountable but are only temporary phenomena. You will go through, under, over or around them. There is less sense of effort even if you're "working hard."

With commitment you are focused. Your attention, conscious or unconscious, is always alert, whether you are asleep or awake. Many solutions to obstacles can occur in sleep. When I decided to give a series of talks in a new country, I woke up out of a sound sleep with five subjects in my mind. I ran stark naked to my desk and jotted them down. The response was overwhelming.

There is much evil in our world. Evil has little problem with commitment. Evil has great energy and tends to be fearless. Goodness is often timid and wishing to be left alone in peace.

A young woman of 16 years of age came to see me. She was referred to me by Dr Al Lowen, the developer of bio-energetic analysis. Al had been my teacher and therapist, and I wanted to do very well with the patient he referred to me. It was a nightmare. It was worse than having your teeth pulled. Nothing worked. Just as I was getting ready to tell her that she should be seeing somebody else, something positive would happen. We dragged on this way for over a year. It was a year of massive frustration. Then she came to the end of her school year. She realised that in one more year she would be finished with her secondary education and wanted to leave home and go to college. She knew she was too weak to be able to leave her domineering mother. Suddenly, everything worked. I was a brilliant therapist. Her responses were immediate, intense, healing, clarifying. She was accepted by an excellent college, confident that she could stand on her own two feet.

When a patient demands of me, "Doctor, tell me what to do," "Doctor, fix me," I know that they are not yet committed to their healing. With commitment, the patient spontaneously starts to move forward in their own healing and allows me to assist with any unseen barriers. Your commitment needs to be focused on the end result, not the path. The path may require changes. A successful entrepreneur once told me, "Everything works out for me, but never quite the way I expected."

When commitment is clearly absent LOOK FOR THE FOOT ON THE BRAKE without being judgemental toward anything you find.

Look and discover your inner compass of awareness. We all have what I call an inner compass in our bodies, in our chest and belly, that points us toward the truth.

Practice body compass awareness with a few obvious sentences "I am a communist." See how you feel. "I am not a communist."

See how you feel. Sense the different reactions in your body between the two sentences.

"I love Brussels sprouts." Pause, sense your body. "I detest Brussels sprouts." Pause, sense your body.

Leave a short pause after each sentence to tune into your body awareness.

Sometimes a sentence will feel comfortable, like putting on a glove that fits perfectly. Sometimes there is a tingling feeling in various parts of your body that tells you that whatever you are thinking or saying is the truth. A profound and newly discovered truth can sometimes result in a temporary altered state of consciousness.

Here are some techniques for promoting awareness and commitment – desire.

Dream Programming. Just before you go to sleep, there is a point where you are partly asleep and partly awake. Your unconscious is very close to your waking state at that point. Have a picture of something you desire, make a brief, poetic phrase of your desire or a step you need to take toward your desire. Picture the phrase or the image for five, ten or fifteen seconds as you fall asleep.

Here are a series of sentences that I tested before I found the correct one:

"I will be like Albert Einstein" – somehow that doesn't feel right.

"I will release my creativity" – that feels better.

"I will become aware of all blocks to my creativity" – this touches me; it produces a feeling in my chest. I feel like I put something on my body that feels comfortable, pleasurable and fits perfectly.

Try this for six weeks and see what happens. At times, even the content of your dreams will help produce clear awareness.

Forehead Writing. Use the same kind of phrases as in the previous exercise, and with an imaginary light, imprint your sentence or your picture on your forehead.

Harvey R. Wasserman

Non-Dominant Handwriting. Write the place where you feel stuck in a clear, brief, poignant sentence. Then keep on writing. Do not concern yourself about the logic or illogic of what you write. Just keep writing for ten, fifteen minutes, and very often a dim light of clarity will start to appear.

Refer to the section on the ego-alien technique in Chapter 18. It can also be useful in eliminating the barriers to commitment.

In the navy, I was in an electronics training programme that made you the equivalent of a sergeant when you graduated. I studied reasonably hard and was usually somewhere near the bottom of my class in my grades. The war ended, and they announced that only the top 10% of people with high grades would be promoted. I wanted it desperately. I went from the bottom of the class to tenth, to eighth, to second, without increasing the effort I put in on study. Desire and commitment removed the blocks to my success.

The Power Of Negative Affirmations

TO ACKNOWLEDGE a weakness or an area of dysfunction – *WITHOUT SELF-CONDEMNATION* – that you're not ready to change, is a sign of awareness and strength, often more powerful and freeing than a positive affirmation. It is a readily available platform for change when the committed decision to change is made.

You know you should meditate, and you don't. Usually you think, "I will meditate tomorrow morning," and you forget and the next, and the next, morning. Read the following statements. After each one, check if there is a confirmatory reaction in your mind and body.

"I don't want to meditate" – no reaction.

"I refuse to admit that I don't want to meditate" – no reaction.

"No one can make me admit that I don't want to meditate" – a smile and change of feeling in your mind.

A crack in the door of denial has opened. Awareness is the beginning of potential change.

Here is a clinical example. A 23-year-old man suffered from low self-esteem, anxiety, poor body image. He was hypercritical of self and others, resulting in very limited social contacts. He made some progress and paid a visit home to a mother he didn't like. Returning to treatment, all signs of improvement were lost. He reported that he had been grinding his teeth.

"Any dreams that stand out?"

He reported a series of dreams in which he was murdered.

"Say with eye contact, 'Harvey, I was afraid my mother could kill me.'"

Confusion, confusion, "You want me to say that?" He changed the subject. Finally, in a soft monotone, he repeated the sentence.

"Any reaction? True, slightly true or not true?"

No reaction.

"Say with eye contact, 'I refuse to admit I was afraid my mother could kill me.' "

No reaction.

"Say, 'Harvey you will never convince me that I was afraid my mother could kill me.' "

Reaction was a smile, and in a slight trance he reported his vision cloudy and a shift to a heavy feeling in his head.

The smile is an opening crack in the wall of denial.

Two minutes later he said, "My mother chased me with a butcher knife and threatened to throw me out of the window."

"Well?"

"But that happened all through my childhood. I never got scared until she threw hammers at my father's head."

Murder In Death Valley

THERE IS ALWAYS a huge Jim Bowie knife and scabbard around my waist whenever I travel in wilderness.

After seven amazing days running the rapids in the Grand Canyon, my wife and I decided to visit Death Valley. It was the spring (no tourists). Night was falling as we entered the canyon. We drove by an intriguing, sensually undulating side canyon. It was too late to explore. We were looking for the only motel that remained open at this time of year. As we settled in our room, a dark, moonlit night surrounded us.

"Something out there wants to kill me," I said. "I just feel or know that something out there wants to kill me."

"You must go out there and confront it."

"I know you're right."

I walked alone for half a mile into the flat central desert. There was nothing there to kill me.

Back at the motel, I told her that whatever wanted to kill me was in that striking narrow canyon we passed as we drove in.

I left her in the car at the canyon mouth. It was mine to walk in, alone.

The high, undulating, sensual walls threw beautiful, terrifying, strange shadows.

I walked to the first bend. I knew my killer was around that bend. I screwed up all my courage and walked around. No one. Only more of the same.

Deeper in the canyon, a second meaningful curve. *My killer is around this one.* I screwed up all my courage and walked around. No one.

Three, four and five were exactly the same. I probably had penetrated three-quarters of a mile into the canyon.

I became terrified. I let myself go crazy. I pulled out my Jim Bowie. Holding it at the attack above my head, I raced around the canyon curve, shouting like a mad man, "I will kill you, you dirty rotten bastard!"

Around the curve, no one. Just me. Harvey was the killer.

I gently placed my Bowie in the scabbard. In complete peace, I strolled back to the canyon mouth, thoroughly enjoying the sculptural effect of the night shadows.

Paranoia True And False

IN THE 1970s I paid a travel agent in Lima, Peru, to arrange a trip to Iquitos on the upper Amazon and then to visit a jungle camp and several tribal peoples.

On arriving in Iquitos, I went to the broken-down hotel. They had never heard of me and had not received payment confirmation. The same response came from the man who was to take me exploring.

I demanded a room, and they finally agreed – it was filled with someone else's possessions. The hotel demanded payment.

I was in a remote, deteriorated town. No one who cared about me knew I was there. Had I fallen into the hands of evil?

There is a killer in me under my civilised exterior. The hotel manager saw it when he said it was not possible to call Lima and confirm my arrangements.

I demanded the call be put through. I was dangerous but controlled.

Alarmed, he put the call through. Contact was made.

The line was so bad it was useless. The problem was inability to communicate.

I realised they weren't lying. I relaxed, repaid everybody and had a wonderful trip.

I learned that paranoia was designed to arm and alert you when there are signs of external possible danger, with no correcting information. Once corrective information is available, paranoia disappears and all is well.

In pathological paranoia, the danger is internally generated; therefore, corrective information is seen as a threat.

Harvey R. Wasserman

Benny Was A Genius

BENNY FINALLY DID IT. He found the money Fay was hiding for their children's education and spent it. After years of losing on the horses, unable to pay rent and having furniture repossessed, he finally did it. Fay, who loved Benny, frequently claimed Benny was a genius. But this was the unforgivable act. She was seriously considering leaving her genius.

Benny definitely did not want to lose Fay. He had an idea. He needed money but had borrowed and lost money from all his friends and relatives — thank God, except one.

Ice cream parlours are a New York speciality. These are places where people go for malteds, sodas, all kinds of ice cream and cake. Benny bought one and redecorated it with a railroad theme. O-gauge model trains ran from the counter to the customer. Orders were placed on a train, taken to the counter and returned fulfilled on a flatbed car.

Success was immediate. Television, newspaper articles, lots of money. Before he could be copied, Benny sold out at a huge profit. The profit was invested in a card and candle shop in a growing affluent community on Long Island.

Success was immediate. Benny sold out at a huge profit and bought a deteriorated department store and revitalised it.

During this time of expansion, my only contact with Benny and his family was through other family members.

Now thirty years go by and I am established in my psychiatric practice. I invite Benny and Fay to my new home. They arrive in the biggest Cadillac I have ever seen. Fay presents herself in a gorgeous mink coat. At lunch Benny discusses fine wines and utters these immortal words, "When the ash tray in my Caddy gets full, I trade it in."

When they left I laughed and laughed. By God, Benny was a genius.

Outback By The Billabong

I WANTED to meet Mandarg, the "very clever fellow" (medicine man) in Arnheim Land, Northern Australia. Arnheim Land is an Aboriginal reserve forbidden to visitors.

I used my Yale connections; no result. One of my patients was a world famous photographer. The Australian travel bureau wanted him to take publicity pictures in Arnheim Land. They were unable to get him in.

Finally I contacted the guide who had taken me into the wilds of New Guinea. He came from an old prominent Australian family. His brother-in-law was the professor of public health at Sydney University College of Medicine. The professor invited me to lunch the next day to make certain my head was screwed on.

I didn't think anyone would take my real reason for the trip seriously, so I told him instead that I wanted to study right and left brain differences in Aboriginal peoples. I knew nothing about right and left brain differences, but neither did anyone else in 1973, so I wouldn't be asked any embarrassing questions. Besides, it sounded scientific.

The next day I was on a plane to Darwin, the city in northern Australia closest to Arnheim Land. The female mayor of Darwin met me at the airport and arranged for a cocktail party. She wanted me to meet important people in Darwin.

The next day the mayor needed an escort to the annual military ball at the massive army base that protects northern Australia. I only had jeans, nice leather runners and a ruffled wedding shirt. The mayor said, "That will do."

In the beautiful moonlight I was seated with the admirals and generals, quite an experience for an ex-seaman first class, World War II vintage. They were nice guys to chat with. One admiral even offered me a take-off and landing on Australia's only aircraft carrier if I was free when it returned to home base. We were waited on by lieutenants, and I danced with the mayor.

　　　　　　　　　　　Harvey R. Wasserman

The next day she arranged an appointment with a lawyer who spoke for Aboriginal chieftains of Arnheim Land. Instead of being a politician he drove a taxi because he couldn't create his ideals of fairness and law as a legislator. The Aboriginals trusted him because he was a taxi driver. He arranged for the chieftains to look me over at a meeting with government officials who wanted to mine uranium on Aboriginal land. The chieftains were shown films about uranium and atomic energy. I passed their indirect observation, but was not successful in meeting Mandarg. They would have had to meet me individually and escort me through their territories. I had to return to the US before they returned to their individual kingdoms.

The next morning I was on a plane of the Australian public health service to Arnheim Land. The health service people asked me a favour. The public health officials wanted me to find out why a schizophrenic girl was hitting her mother, which was very unusual behaviour among Aboriginals. The family lived in a wilderness area just outside of the Owen-Pele Mission Station. The missionaries had left years before. The Australian health people had built a magnificent, fully equipped modern hospital in Owen-Pele and then decided it was cheaper to fly patients to their hospital in Darwin. Staff quarters were built and available, so there was a place for me to stay.

I was met at the landing strip by Isaiah. He spoke pretty good English, having attended a missionary school before the missionaries left. After settling me in the unused staff quarters, he took me on a tour of the abandoned hospital.

Driving me back to my quarters we passed the church, a large building with a huge painting of Jesus in the usual posture across the front of the building.

"That's Jesus. Jesus was a Jew." He said this in the sing-song manner of a child who has memorised something he doesn't understand.

Among Australian Aboriginals, whom you are related to is of enormous importance. I was quiet for a few moments. I always am when someone mentions Jew.

Finally I said, "I am a Jew."

"You're a Jew?"

"Yes."

"You're one of his people?"

"Yes."

"You're one of his tribe?"

"Yes."

In a state of awe he fell silent, unable to speak to me for the rest of my stay. He was in the presence of a relative of God. He would do anything for me but could not speak. He was helping a member of God's family.

Isaiah knew I was supposed to visit the Aboriginal family with a disturbed daughter. The next day he pointed me down a narrow trail at the edge of Owen-Pele village.

I walked for about thirty minutes to a clearing in the jungle. There was a large thatched building with a leaf-covered clearing at its front. Present was an oldish man who was painting while sitting on the ground. Sitting on a box was an oldish woman watching the many children. She also was watching a young woman who appeared to be in her twenties. The young woman was staring intensely at the children at play.

I introduced myself to the gentleman I assumed to be the father. I explained that the health service had sent me because they were worried about his daughter. He received me silently and pleasantly but continued with his painting. It was a beautiful painting similar to the ones I had seen in the Sydney museum. I subsequently found out that the finished painting would be taken to a remote area of the closed border and exchanged for a bottle of whiskey.

We sat in silence. I pulled out some paper and pen that I happened to have with me and drew a picture of a totem animal that I had received at a shamanistic workshop in the US. My rendition was of a bear with an eagle on its head. It brought an enthusiastic response: "Your father's dream."

In the silence of our painting, his comment drew us closer even though I didn't have a clue as to what he meant. I knew

Harvey R. Wasserman

that in Aboriginal culture "dream time" was their spiritual world.

I stayed with my host for several hours working at our paintings and observing their family behaviour. I stayed away from the women. I didn't know what the cultural norm was about such things. If you get it wrong in some cultures, you can get yourself into a lot of trouble, even killed.

After two hours I knew why the girl was hitting her mother. Whenever the children had a problem, they ran to grandma. Mama would go into a silent rage. There was no hitting while I was there.

I asked my host how old his daughter was. He stunned me when he said, "I do not know when women are born."

After about three hours, our paintings were finished. I had discovered what I came for and left them with a departing gift, a Polaroid picture of the family.

I lined up the family, dad, mum, daughter and six children. They were delighted with the new experience until I developed the film. The schizophrenic daughter's part of the emulsion stuck. She was not in the group photo of her family! They were terrified. For them something terrible, even magical and mystical, had happened. My explanations had no effect. I managed a second picture in which they all appeared. This had no effect. I returned to the Owen-Pele village leaving behind a terrified family who had seen black magic at work.

The Health Service flew me back to Darwin. I delivered my report, then went on to Melbourne.

Shortly after I checked into my hotel in Melbourne I received a phone call from the secretary of the most important financial figure in Australia. She wanted to set up a phone conversation time with me and her boss for the next day. He couldn't talk to me on my arrival day because he was being given a gold medal by the Australian government.

"Oh my God! He must want to know what I had discovered about right and left brain differences in Aboriginal culture." I knew nothing but one thing: a book had recently been published.

The thirtieth bookstore I called in Melbourne had one copy. A long taxi ride, and I had it. I stayed up all night studying what turned out to be a very fat book.

Australia's financial hero called me the next day. He had heard I was an expert on the relationship between Aboriginal and Western peoples. I assured him that he was misinformed, and we said a polite goodbye.

A little research discovered two amazing natural phenomena near Melbourne, the giant earth worms and the fairy penguins.

As you drive south from Melbourne to visit the homecoming of the fairy penguins, you pass through a mysterious unmarked area, one of two places on earth where there are giant earthworms. Some are over ten feet long and six inches in diameter. There is no way to see them. You have to put your ear to the ground. Listen to them munching through the earth.

On to the penguins. You need a reservation and will be given a specific time to arrive. The rangers will place you in a specific spot so that the route to the nests is not blocked. Stand for fifteen to twenty minutes before anything happens. The rangers know the exact time of arrival.

Out of the foam of low-breaking waves, a series of six or eight small creatures will materialise and waddle ashore, staggering, their protruding bellies stuffed with the day's fish catch. They squeal and squawk as they stagger uphill, noisier as they bump into each other and try to find the right path to their nest. You are an alien giant ignored in a natural world that is amazing, amusing and beyond cute.

Harvey R. Wasserman

CHAPTER THREE

EMOTIONS

"Harvey, You Don't Have To Worry About Going To Hell - This Is It"

SHE WAS STANDING on a chair, one arm reaching to a high kitchen shelf. She did not reply when I spoke to her. Her body, arm and face – frozen like a statue. She was catatonic, a severe form of schizophrenia.

I don't know how long she was that way when I came home from my office. In my terror, I don't know how long she remained that way until she moved and spoke. That very morning I left a lovely, normal, happy and emotionally present wife. On returning to the living world from catatonia, she descended into a deep depression. It was 1957 — 7 years of happy marriage. Our lives would never be the same again.

I had been treating her father for manic depressive illness that erupted in his forties, after we were married. The disease usually comes on suddenly between the ages of 19 to 25. Her father had refused help from anyone else.

She withdrew from the world, stayed in bed until 2 pm or 3 pm. She listened to the radio a lot and wrote endlessly on paper, not on the lines but in circles. She could enjoy movies, theatre, adventurous vacations but was always late, inconveniencing everybody.

One beautiful, freezing morning, sixty below zero in Yellowstone Park in winter, she kept our friends waiting in the freezing cold before she was ready to begin our daily cross-country ski adventures.

I sent her to every psychiatrist and therapist of reputation. No one helped. In one of Dr. Al Lowen's books her case is anonymously presented as cured. The only change was that she no longer believed there was anything wrong with her.

Her teeth painfully deteriorated, and most of them had to be pulled. She refused to return to the dentist when her temporary teeth were to be replaced. They deteriorated, and she

Harvey R. Wasserman

glued them together with tape from Band-aids. When she showed her temporary teeth, they were all black.

I tried to get her working with me. Friends tried to bring her out of the house, to little avail.

There were outbursts of rage. She began to wander around the house most nights, wailing like a banshee. At one point I hadn't had a night's sleep for three months. At my Yale office the colours in paintings seemed to move. I was in sleep deprivation hallucination. I decided that to survive I would have to leave. She sensed that and stopped. I knew I would leave if she ever started again.

We had an argument about food being allowed to rot in the refrigerator. I fled from the house. She followed and grabbed a .22 calibre rifle I had in a closet. It was loaded and on safety; an escaped murderer had been in our area. As I ran to the car, a bullet whistled by my ear.

She damaged several items I treasured, a beautiful carving I brought back from New Guinea, a beautiful Zuni Indian neck piece given to me by friends on my fiftieth birthday. I saw her do this. She denied it.

Three years after she had stopped wandering and wailing, she began again. I couldn't leave. I found her on the floor, wailing. I embraced her to comfort her and felt murderous hate come from her body. She wanted to kill me!

I fled for my life with the clothes on my back and in desperation found super strength to lift a filing cabinet into my car so I could carry on with my life.

I fled, never to return. I had stayed thirty-three years too long.

Both my sons have something similar to her.

I Will Never Be Happy Again

I WILL NEVER be happy again; the good times are over. I am standing at the door of my grandparents' living room staring at my grandmother's coffin. The coffin is on two sawhorses, the mirrors and pictures are covered. Like a film negative, all I see is in black and white, except that what should be black is white, and what is white should be black.

I am four years old. I am in shock. No one is talking to me. I don't understand what happened. I know it is dire. My fear of disaster, my fear of being alone and abandoned, much of all my fears began that night.

I am sick on the living room couch. I feel terrible. My mama, she doesn't come. Grandma comes and lovingly comforts me. No memory of my father exists at that time. My grandfather is a series of unpleasant memories.

I forgot I had a grandmother. Forty years later at a therapy workshop, the reverse negative image returned. I couldn't remember my grandmother's name. I called my sister. MIRIAM. I couldn't remember Miriam unless I called my sister.

Telling or writing or reading this story brings tears to my eyes and agony to my body and clouds to my consciousness.

I have been talking lovingly to little Harvey. The negative starts to reverse, and finally a full colour picture appears.

I have known that I must talk to my grandma each night. I must revisit all of this each night until I heal.

Harvey R. Wasserman

Instant Happiness

FOR FIVE MINUTES walk around your room or house with the eyes of a baby, that is, seeing everything, every object, even a crack or a spot on the wall, with no judgment – non-judgemental.

Nothing is reacted to as good or bad, beautiful or ugly.

Now for five minutes walk around with a feeling with love for everything – that spot, that crack, the fly on the wall, the lamp - everything.

For five minutes walk around with an attitude of gratitude for everything that comes into your visual field, including all the above.

If you don't feel calmer and happier, I will be very surprised.

Balancing The Emotions

EMOTIONS CAN ENRICH, damage, or destroy your life. Emotions are psychological and biological events. When this essential part of your humanity is in balance, your intellect becomes a more useful and reliable tool.

Emotion comes from the Latin meaning, "to move out." In this vital exercise the sound of each emotion is an effective and convenient way to express and bring your emotions into balance.

With each emotion, bring it up consciously if you can, or remember an incident that evoked that emotion. Make a sound that seems to come from the emotion. Sustain the sound and repeat it for about ninety seconds, then take three deep, cleansing breaths and go to the next emotion. The main emotions are:

- Fear
- Anger
- Emotional Pain
- Sadness
- Love
- Joy
- Sexuality / Sensuality
- Spirituality

For spirituality, make the sound of the letter E and then raise its pitch higher and higher until there is no audible sound, only a breath sound. Three or four times, lower the pitch to an audible range and then raise it up to the breath sound. You should feel as if something is moving through and out the top of your head.

How do you feel? You probably have a sense of well-being.

Harvey R. Wasserman

If you want to intensify the effect, listen to some deeply relaxing music after the emotional series.

Another way to improve the effect is to have something like a large eraser, something that is firm but will give a little, with pressure. Have it on a comfortable surface next to your chair and touch it with your index finger, pressing down and slightly forward, in a pattern that seems to express the emotion as you are doing the sound emotion. Fear is contraction, so the physical expression should be down and backward.

If done at least two to three times a week, this healing experience can be extremely beneficial in improving emotional problems. There have also been reports that frequent practice for many months has improved some medical problems.

It is important when you do this not just to do the difficult emotions, but to make sure that you have time to complete the entire series.

The Curse Of Depression

HAVE YOU EVER AWAKENED one morning with a feeling of low energy, not really wanting to get out of bed, not wanting to do very much, pessimistic about your life? Your low mood may have lasted a few hours, a day or even several days. If it's severe depression, you actually may not get out of bed, or you may not be able to get yourself to do anything.

The symptoms of depression are a loss of energy, a loss of interest in many important aspects of life, and a decrease in hope about the future. Your mind is preoccupied with negative thoughts about yourself and your environment. There may be a loss of appetite or massive overeating. Insomnia or long hours in bed are common. You probably stay up late and sleep late.

What causes human beings to descend into that state of hell called depression? There are many. By far the most common causes of depression are when powerful emotions are buried. Emotions are psychological events with biological components. They are powerful sources of energy that, if not discharged, can cause problems.

The most common cause of depression that I see in Ireland is emotional pain. Emotional pain arises when hurt is done to the part of us that loves – your heart. When this hurt is powerful, is beyond our awareness, or is not discharged, it shuts down the life force.

Emotional pain is not the only emotion that can cause this level of misery. This misery can be caused by any of the emotions. The main emotions are fear, anger, emotional pain, sadness, love, joy, sexuality/sensuality and spirituality. All mishandled emotions can produce depression.

Depression is a universal human phenomenon. There are times of well-being, and times of mild depression in most people. Depression is a syndrome (a collection of symptoms) not a disease in itself. It has many causes.

Harvey R. Wasserman

Depression can be caused by toxins, such as copper poisoning. It can be caused by cerebral allergies, commonly to wheat or milk. It can be caused by medical illness, such as hypothyroidism. Brain tumours can cause depression. Brain deterioration can appear first as depression.

Epilepsy is usually thought of as causing convulsions of the muscles, but in one type of epilepsy the electrical disorder is in parts of the brain that have to do with emotions and can thus appear as depression.

Many viruses, even the common flu, can cause depression. There are genetic depressions such as manic depressive illness. Failure of psychotherapeutic and biochemical treatment of depression is often due to ignorance of the underlying cause.

By far the main cause of depression is psychological. Some of these can be treated with psychotherapy. When a basic belief system at the centre of somebody's life proves to be false, depression is often the result. "If I am a good, loving wife, my partner will be faithful." "I always wanted to be a musician, but I'm trapped in a salaried job." Often the best treatment is short-term use of anti-depressants, along with powerful and deep psychotherapy.

Let me give you some examples.

Case No. 1. This is from my own life. When I reached the age of 40, I went through a mild depression. I was leading a successful life, was a professor at Yale, had a busy and lucrative private practice, a nice home, great vacations, a wife and two children. Yet at times my energy level was down. I was frequently preoccupied with negative thoughts, including thoughts about death. Finally I discovered why. At the age of 40 I had lived and carried out all the tasks of life that my mother had programmed in me. I had finished my programming. It took me about two years to find new directions in my life that expressed who I, Harvey, really was. Once I did that, the depression disappeared.

Case No. 2. A 40-year-old handsome and intelligent woman was more than moderately depressed. She had two lovely children and a stable marriage. Her husband was a good man who worked hard, supported her and did not abuse her or the children in any way. But she needed somebody to share her emotions with, a friend whom she could intimately communicate with. This was not her husband. This caused her extreme pain. She descended into depression. In psychotherapy she realised her marriage was totally unsatisfactory. She began a self-supporting career and divorced her husband, not in anger but for her emotional well-being.

Case No 3. A uniquely Irish depression occurred in a man who was religious and brilliant. It took six months to figure out his depression: "Everything is easy for me – everyone else struggles and suffers." He felt a true Christian should struggle and suffer. It took a few months to convince him that being gifted – a genius – was nothing to be arrogant about or ashamed of, but to be humbly appreciated and used. His depression thankfully vanished.

If you choose to look for buried emotion, simply say out loud, "I don't want to feel my fear." Pause, repeat with pain, then repeat about anger, sadness, love, joy, sensuality, and spirituality. If you sense a body or mind indication that an emotion is strong and well-hidden, there are self-help books and treatment programs that can teach you to release the dammed-up emotions causing your suffering.

(See *Balancing the Emotions,* in this Chapter.)

Research has shown that aerobic exercise about 25 minutes a day produces measurable positive changes in brain chemistry, relieving depression.

A closed heart permits you to function but removes much of the joy of life, resulting in a kind of mild depression. Place the palm of your hand on the middle of your sternum or breast bone, about 1/3 of the length of your sternum from the bottom of the sternum. Eyes closed, imagine this place under your palm for one minute — then in the same place imagine a most beautiful scene for one minute. This should result in a strong, pleasurable feeling of happiness. Your closed heart has just opened. Repeating this exercise will put you on the path to an open heart.

See *The Heart Roots Exercise* and *The Heart Chant* in Chapter 11.

Harvey R. Wasserman

Depression Diagnosis: Circular Breathing

IF YOU FEEL depressed for no known reason and it's due to an unaware emotional or thought process, try the following:

Notice that in normal breathing there is a brief pause at the end of breathing in and at the end of breathing out. For one or two minutes, consciously eliminate this very brief pause. It requires concentration; it is a type of hyperventilation.

Give yourself 30 to 40 seconds to settle down when you stop.

Do you sense an emotion or thought process that you were not conscious of before?

If you can glance in a mirror, you might see a facial expression you are not conscious of. A sensitive companion who observes you after circular breathing may be able to pick up some of the above, even if you yourself are not aware.

This technique is not always successful, but it is simple, safe and worth a try.

Despair

DESPAIR IS THE MOST AWFUL emotional state one can experience. Life is hardly worth living. Despair is often accompanied by suicidal thoughts. When there is despair without a glimmer of hope, suicidal behaviour is a definite possibility.

Try out this sentence:

"At an early age I found life so painful that I would only stay here in this world because I knew I could always escape through suicide."

More simply:

"Often suicide seems the only escape from the despair of life."

If your response is, "That's me," you may be what is called switched. Switching is a concept developed in applied kinesiology. Switching is a distortion in the nervous system. Switching affects decisions and distorts the personality, particularly decisions that relate to major life choices, especially intimate ones.

Switching can be temporarily corrected by a circular massage with the palm of the hand through the clothes over the belly button, which stimulates two acupuncture points on either side of the belly button. With the palm of the other hand, it's easy to use a gentle circular stimulation of an acupuncture point that exists at the beginning of the first thoracic intraspace adjacent to the sternum, just below the clavicle. There is such a point on each side of the chest. The direction of palm rotation is irrelevant. Do not allow the upper palm to slide down! (Make certain your thumb lightly touches the neck.)

When this is accomplished for about forty-five seconds, the next step is to cross-crawl — simultaneously bending joints on opposite sides of the body; for example, first the right leg and left arm, and then the left leg and right arm. This is believed to improve communication across the centre of the brain, the corpus callosum.

Usually only ninety seconds is necessary to complete this part of the technique. Then walk around. You will feel more positive, stronger, in better contact with the ground. Repeat this several times per day or whenever you feel bad. Unswitching keeps any creative work or decision much more likely to come to fruition, so unswitching work is very desirable.

Severe persistent despair is dangerous and should have trained professional attention.

Awareness And Healing, The Surrender Technique

LIE ON YOUR BACK on a firm mattress. Let the top third of your chest, as well as your head, hang down backward as far as possible. Stretch your hands straight up from your shoulders and let them hang down as far as possible. Bend your knees so that the bottoms of your feet are flat on the mattress.

Take in a deep breath and blow it out all the way. Repeat two times. Hold your breath out the third time. Hold it out as long as you possibly can and fill your mind with the thoughts, "I give up; I surrender; no more struggling; no more, no more."

When you absolutely have to breathe, sit up immediately and see if you sense any thoughts, memories or emotions that you were unaware of before the exercise. Stay with this new awareness until your body relaxes to normal. It is useful to have a hand mirror nearby. You may be able to see facial expressions that have not yet reached consciousness.

Repeat this exercise two more times. Particularly on the third time, hold your breath as long as you possibly can, hopefully even longer than before.

Usually you will find that any negative memories, emotions or attitudes that came up during the first or second parts of the exercise are improved after the third repetition.

Doing this series of exercises on a regular basis can be a powerful self-help technique and a boost to any ongoing psychotherapy.

An acute observer may see an important and powerful emotional-facial reaction still under the surface of conscious awareness.

The Hagen Handshake

LINDBLAD TRAVEL is a most innovative travel company. They initiated the first tourist group to the New Guinea highlands in the 1970s. The first white explorers made it up into the highlands in the 1930s.

Margaret Mead, the anthropologist, said, "If you want to see the Stone Age, go to New Guinea now." I went with Lindblad. It was too dangerous to go alone. The locals were still beheading and eating each other.

Half way up the steep bulldozed mountain roads of New Guinea, we ran into an landslide that blocked the road to the small town of Mount Hagen.

Wherever in the world I have stopped on a remote jungle road, out of the dark forest of trees appear natives, always carrying a machete. This time was no exception as we waited for our rescue bulldozer.

A native woman and her teenage daughter walked up to my wife. The native woman rubbed my wife's genitals.

"Harvey! What does she want?"

"I don't know, maybe she goes for you," was my reply.

Our guide, a distinguished Englishman, came over and explained that my wife had just experienced the Hagan Handshake, an expression of greeting or admiration or thank you among the Hagen people.

"She is admiring your long hair. The local women mostly have curly short hair and admire women with long hair."

He then explained that he first encountered the Hagen Handshake the previous month when two elderly native women gently rubbed his testicles. Being very British, he acted cool, as if nothing unusual had happened.

To the Hagen people, it is a friendly genital greeting, including hello, thank you and goodbye. These are not sexual overtures, nor are there any sexual overtones, only a basic wish for your health, prosperity, and especially, fertility. The Hagen Handshake takes a while for Westerners to get used to, but eventually seems pleasantly friendly.

The mountains of New Guinea are steep and separate one valley from the next. Each valley has individual cultural traits and separate languages. There are over five hundred languages in New Guinea. The Hagen people are aggressive, and the men always carry a stone axe. Although their greeting is genital, in most ways their behaviour is punitive and conservative. For example, if you are unfaithful to your husband, you lose your nose!

The very next day, I had my own encounter with the Hagen Handshake.

Too Frightened To Say "You're Welcome"

AS A CHILD, I thought my parents lived a very dull life. My father worked long hours at his job, a job he hated. My mother took care of the house and the kids. She really wanted to be a writer. There was little else in their lives.

There was enough money, even during the Great Depression, for me to go to the movies every week.

There was a double feature every Saturday for only ten cents. What was more important were the adrenalin serials "Buck Rogers in the 25th Century," or "Frank Buck's *Bring 'Em Back Alive.*" They provided twenty to twenty-five minutes of great adventure ending with the threat of annihilation of our hero. You had to return the next Saturday to find out how he survived and then went into his endless next adventure and threat to his survival.

I was determined to have a life with excitement and adventure.

In 1971 I was in a remote area of the Hagen Valley in New Guinea, a place where the Stone Age still survives. Walking down a jungle trail by myself, I came to a clearing with a garden of sweet potatoes and a primitive thatched hut. Sweet potatoes 3-4 ft long were the staple diet of the natives.

Out of the hut came an elderly gentleman. (They rarely live beyond forty years of age.) I greeted him with my few words of pidgin English, a mixture of English and Dutch. I admired his homestead and gifted him with a piece of candy. (Sweets are scarce in jungle areas. The bees give up their honey with great reluctance.)

He was delighted. He reached between my legs with his open hand and rubbed my testicles.

I had already become acquainted with the Hagen Handshake. I knew the appropriate courteous "You're welcome" was to reach between his legs, palm open, and rub his testicles.

I was wearing jeans and underpants. He only wore a carved bark belt and some leaves stuffed down the front and back. (The Australians call this ass grass.) Nothing was over his testicles!

I flattened my palm, bent my elbow and started to reach between his legs. Halfway there, my arm froze. Energised by the fear in my chest and belly, I raised my arm and patted him on the back.

Maybe I would never be Buck Rogers in the 25th Century or Bring 'Em Back Alive Frank Buck.

Where Are The Eternal Truths?

EVERY WOMAN is a prostitute in a small community on the Sepik River of New Guinea.

Their houses are built on poles to keep them out of the water. Their backyard is a log platform raised behind their home. Each home is occupied by a family.

Marriages are stable, children play, seem happy and are loved. They keep a few chickens and beat an edible powder out of the core of certain palm trees. Everything else is acquired by barter.

Female sexuality is the currency for obtaining other food-stuffs and implements. Every little girl will grow up and con-tribute to her family.

Life is peaceful and seems quite normal after you hang around for a while. Immorality is nowhere in the atmosphere.

Trading With The Natives

WE WERE LOST in our car while following a vague trail in a remote area of Kenya.

A Masai warrior herdsman and forty of his cattle blocked our path. After a short, friendly conversation with him in my limited Swahili, I noticed he wore a short sword in a beautifully beaded scabbard.

I whipped out a hundred pound note in trade. He took my bill and examined it slowly and carefully. He compared it with rolled-up paper money that he held in curls on his head. Slightly puzzled, he declined my offer, and we drove on.

Finally we knew we were lost and turned back on the trail before it completely disappeared. On our trip back, we came across our friendly Masai warrior herdsman. He greeted us joyfully by jumping repeatedly.

They stand erect, slim and well-built. They wear a reddish purple robe very similar to a Roman robe, carry a spear, a sword, and walk barefoot. They can stand on one foot for hours. When they jump for joy they jump from a standing position and can achieve what appears to be two feet in height with little or no effort.

I wanted that sword. Inspiration struck. I pulled out 10 ten-pound notes, which he received with joy. The deal was consummated.

Harvey R. Wasserman

CHAPTER FOUR

AVOIDING THE TRUE SELF

Rob
Destiny And Death

Rob

ROB WAS A DEVOUT protestant minister. He was spiritual leader of a small congregation near Boston. A Christian psychotherapy centre was treating his wife, but referred Rob to me to help him with his anxiety.

Rob was a nice but dull man and a devout Christian. He had courted a beautiful communist girl when he was in divinity school. One night she invited him to her apartment. At last he knew his lust would be satisfied. In the taxi she asked if he believed in God. A no meant yes, and a yes meant no. Rob said, "Yes."

When he came to see me, his anxiety centred on his reaction to his wife's growing independence, a product of her psychotherapy.

As soon as I started to work with Rob, strange things began to happen. Lights and sparkling radiances leapt from his body. At night he reported he was taken out of his body to a school. He knew he was being re-educated but couldn't remember the content in the morning.

His eyes sparkled. His voice became strong and lively. He developed unique abilities. He could read people's minds and emotions. He could see and describe people at a distance. I tested him by having him speak to a very distinctive woman I knew. While talking to her over the telephone, Rob described her with unbelievable accuracy, including the clothes she was wearing. We both were amazed.

To ground him, I introduced him to people I knew who were schooled in nonconventional reality. In one of these meetings, he told a doctor that the doctor's wife (who was a stranger to Rob) was about to go into psychotherapy practice with a psychologist. He warned that this could lead to the wife's suicide.

I knew the psychologist was a bit mad and definitely nasty. I also knew from confidential sources that he had previously had an affair with the doctor's wife. Taking Rob's warning to heart, the doctor talked his wife out of the partnership.

Rob told his bishop of his unusual experiences and unexpectedly received the bishop's blessing.

Rob accepted a young female divinity student into his church. They fell in love. I already knew his marriage was an unhappy one.

At this point, his treatment with me was over. Rob invited me to visit his ancestral home on the island of Lewis and Harris in the Scottish Hebrides.

At the same time, his amazing evolution became too much for Rob. He sent the divinity student away, decided to stay with his wife, and shut down all his new talents. Once more Rob was his old, boring self.

I had already agreed to travel with him. At a cemetery in Lewis in the northern part of the island, where he believed his ancestors were buried, Rob said, "I hear my ancestors calling me." I paid no attention.

Three weeks after we returned to the US, he developed abdominal pain that was diagnosed as untreatable pancreatic cancer.

I researched several alternative treatments for this horrible disease. Rob passively rejected them all. Rob wanted to die.

He was dead eight months later.

Destiny And Death

JULIA WAS a striking, statuesque blonde. Her charisma was powerful. You would notice her presence.

Julia was a woman of leisure. Married to a wealthy businessman, she spent her time playing bridge and enjoying golf. Julia felt guilty about her lifestyle. "I should be doing something to help people, but I don't." Julia was afraid of taking on the responsibility of helping others. Something in her said, *You couldn't handle a life of service to others.*

She came to my office massively terrified from breast cancer with a liver metastasis the size of a small grapefruit.

My job was to minimise her panic. It seemed clear to both of us that her cancer was somehow related to her need to help others and her inability to feel capable of helping them.

After she had calmed down, I took a two-week vacation. Feeling that she still needed support, I referred her to my friend and fellow therapist, Tony. On my return, I also referred her to a famous healer, Olga Worrell.

I first met Olga at a professional meeting. I was having lunch with a young female therapist friend of mine. Olga came for lunch and walked behind the two of us, stopping behind my luncheon companion.

Olga engaged her. "Does the name Florence mean anything to you?"

"Yes," my lunch partner replied. "She is my grandma. She died last week."

"She is standing behind you and asked me to tell you not to worry about your present difficulty. It will turn out ok."

Olga walked on, leaving my companion pale and speechless.

Olga was a dumpy looking, pleasant, middle-aged woman. She claimed to have healed people since childhood. She invited any scientist to test her abilities. A university group in Atlanta discovered she could change the flow of subatomic particles by holding her hands outside a cloud chamber. (A cloud chamber makes visible the path of these particles.) They also tested her ability to do this from 700 miles away. A group at a Canadian university established that Olga could voluntarily change the speed of chemical reactions.

I decided to advise Julia to visit Olga at her healing clinic in Baltimore. The clinic was in a broken-down part of the city in an old church. I had gone there with a medical problem, but I was not healed. Julia had a positive emotional experience in Baltimore but had no obvious medical result.

Shortly after her return she had a dream. In the dream Olga was looking at her with an unusual and profound look in her eyes.

I asked Julia to become the Olga of her dream and create the Olga look in her eyes. When she was ready, I had Julia look at herself, focusing on her eyes in my office mirror.

Suddenly we both saw a blinding flash of white light. I began shaking all over, every part of me. Julia was experiencing the same. I told her I felt sexually excited. Julia admitted she experienced the same. We both knew something important had happened.

After Julia left I called a friend and described what I had experienced. "I am still shaking. It's like fear, but it's not fear."

My friend replied, "That's simple, you're in a state of awe." I knew that she was correct.

The next day Julia was examined by her oncologist. The liver metastasis had disappeared.

Six months went by. Her terror was gone, but the anxiety continued. Julia became increasingly aware of her inner voice saying, *You are living a meaningless life. You should be helping people. People trust you and are drawn to you.*

Her lifestyle did not change. Julia was so terrified of the responsibility of offering her help to others, she couldn't imagine changing direction. This was fed by low self-esteem and became the focus of our work together.

Suddenly, she became very ill. I visited her in the hospital. The staff told me that she was riddled with metastases. There was no hope. When I spoke to Julia she told me in a weak, pleading voice that still brings tears to my eyes, "Harvey, I will change when I get better. I will do what I am supposed to be doing." She died two weeks later.

This is not the end of the Julia story. While I was working with Julia, I took a vacation and sent her to Tony because she was anxious and needed support while I was away. Tony is the least mystical or spiritual person you can imagine. After Julia's brief encounter with Tony, Julia's best friend, a public health nurse, became Tony's patient.

The two weeks following Julia's death were amazing. A 23-year-old patient of mine was in deep despair as she watched her beloved father dying. During the week after Julia died, she came for two appointments with me. Her grief and despair were overwhelming.

A strange, pale beige light filled my office. I knew it was Julia. In thought I asked Julia to comfort my suffering patient. In amazement the patient blurted out, "I feel ok. I feel comforted."

That same week, stunned, Tony told me he saw Julia standing behind her friend during her therapy session. His view of reality was (temporarily) smashed.

The following week Tony told me that his own patient, Julia's best friend, had been giving a public health lecture to an audience full of teenage secondary school students. At the end of her lecture, a young man about 15 years of age approached and accurately described every aspect of Julia, her blonde hair, her statuesque build, her radiance: "She was standing behind you as you lectured.

CHAPTER FIVE

CHERRY PIE

The Attack Of The Cherry Pie
"A Piece Of Cherry Pie," A Short Story

The Attack Of The Cherry Pie

MY PATIENT was having psychotic episodes every morning at about 2 am.

He was just home from having a hernia repaired at the local hospital. In my office, he was sane. When I rushed to his home at 2-3 am, he was sane. What the hell was going on?

I decided to stay all night until I decoded the strange pattern.

What I observed was his wife politely cutting him to ribbons under the guise of being helpful. I then placed a psychiatric nurse in their home with instructions to politely stop the laceration.

(This was the first time that husband and wife had been together full time, in living memory.)

My nurse shared with me her observation of the strange tale of "A Piece Of Cherry Pie."

Harvey R. Wasserman

"A Piece Of Cherry Pie" — A Short Story

"IT CERTAINLY IS NICE to have Martha take dinner with us, isn't it, John?"

"It certainly is nice," he droned in reply.

"I find it relaxing to have someone else here. Not that I mind the strain. It's not that. I can take it. I have always been the strong one. I never know when something is going to happen, though. There's no sense to it. That's what makes it hard. John can seem as normal as he does now, then he suddenly changes. For no reason. You're feeling all right now, John, aren't you?"

"Yes, dear," he replied in careful cadence.

"You're sure, John?"

"I'm sure," he echoed.

"I just want to know for your own good. You're certain you're not feeling funny?"

Again his agreement echoed.

"John, I wouldn't want you to say so just to make me feel better."

"I feel fine, dear," came the reply, carrying an exaggerated note of resignation.

"Well, if you're certain about it" – and she turned from her husband. "Martha, I always take good care of my husband. If there's one thing I am, it's a good nurse. I guess what happened has to do with the operation. John seemed normal in the hospital, though, after the hernia was operated. It first happened on his fourth day home."

She turned to her husband. He was sitting placidly at the dinner table, but with a hint of stiffness – like an Egyptian statue. "Would you like some dessert, dear?"

"No, thank you."

"I have cherry pie."

"No, thank you," came the even reply.

"You know you like my cherry pie, John."

"I'll have a piece, dear." His answers seemed careful.

"Besides," she added, "it's good for you. You need to build up your strength. Martha, being a real nurse, you know how uncomfortable a man can be after an operation. They're not strong like us women. We were sitting around after dinner, and of course, I was trying to make John comfortable. Wasn't I, dear?"

"That's right," the echo replied.

"Then he started to look funny. Kind of glassy, you know. Like he wasn't in the room. John – would you like a large or a small piece of pie?"

"A small piece, dear," he answered.

"How about a large piece. Cherry pie is your favourite."

The knife in her hand was held poised over the pie. She turned her attention to Martha, and didn't seem to hear her husband when he answered, "A small piece will do."

"You wouldn't believe it, Martha, but he started to speak in a loud voice. John *never* speaks in a loud voice. Not in all our thirty married years has he ever raised his voice around me. He said the strangest things. The world is coming to an end! The bomb is going to be dropped! Everyone will be killed! We are all going to die! He seemed to be looking at me. Well, sort of – maybe kind of through me. I was frightened. Well, not really. John wouldn't hurt me. I would never be afraid of that. John – you do want a big piece of pie?"

"That's ok, dear," he answered.

She lifted the knife on the pie, and spoke to her guest. "If there's one thing I know, it's that John wouldn't want to hurt me. What reason would he have? We've always been close. We never go anywhere alone. Always together. That's how close we are. I know John would tell you what a good marriage it's been.

Harvey R. Wasserman

We raised two fine boys, both married and doing well. Is this piece big enough, John?" She measured off a restaurant-sized piece.

"That's fine, dear."

"Of course, I was worried. I called the doctor. He came right over and gave John some pills. Are you sure you don't want a smaller piece?"

There was no reply.

"I want you to have the piece you want. Don't take a big piece just for me. Here, I'll cut you a small one. You're sure that's all you want, though? You can have a bigger piece if you'd really like it. How about this big?" She measured an imaginary piece with her fingers.

John slowly rose from his chair. He moved slowly, stiffly – mechanically – as if the motors of a hidden, mysterious force were lifting him. His face was wooden, his eyes glassy.

"The bombs are falling!"

The End

CHAPTER SIX

FULFILMENT

The Lama Govinda

"LAMA, YOUR BOOKS are on my shelf. I haven't read them. They are like diamonds to me," she said.

I said "Lama, I never knew you wrote a book."

"You have something to look forward to," he replied in his German accent without a trace of egotism.

Virginia Satir, an outstanding psychiatric social worker, formed IHLRN, an organisation of people she believed were creative regardless of background or training. We met once a year to teach and stimulate each other beyond our normal boundaries.

This year we met in Maui, Hawaiian Islands. The first evening Virginia divided us up into groups of eight. In my group was a man dressed in the robes of a Tibetan lama. He became my picture, my model, of mental health. He was the most evolved human being I had ever met or had the privilege to meet. I made sure to spend every moment of our five-day meeting in the company of the Lama Govinda.

The Lama graduated in Germany with a PhD in religion and decided Buddhism was the only religion that made sense. He travelled the world studying, absorbing wisdom from many centres of Buddhist teaching, ending up in Tibet where eventually he achieved the status of lama. A lama has the status of a bishop – not the power, but status in learning and personal evolution.

The lama was found in a hut on a hill top in India by a wealthy member of IHLRN. What the Lama was doing there I don't know, but he was brought food by the locals, who considered him a holy man. Getting older, the lama wanted to return to the West to continue his writing and publishing. He was brought to California and provided with a house and income.

The Lama Govinda was whatever he spoke. I know of no other way to describe what it was like to be in his presence. There was a unity of word usage, facial expression, body posture, body movement, oneness that I have never experienced in anyone else before or since.

There was clarity and wisdom when he spoke, no attempt to manipulate or impress, no subtle diverting overtones. He laughed a lot and his eyes sparkled. He radiated kindness and warmth.

I not only chose to experience his unique presence, I tested him to see if what he seemed was real. I can be pretty sneaky, but he detected all of my tests. He always passed them with a laugh. There are a few I can still remember.

It was Halloween and all participants were requested to wear costumes.

"Lama, you are supposed to wear a costume today."

"I always wear a costume," he said with a little laugh.

"Lama, I always thought that Lamas were people who could do unusual things like reverse the blood flow in their veins."

"If we have any gifts, we don't talk about them," he said softly and in a matter-of-fact manner.

The lama devoted his life to removing negativity from his being. I think he achieved that goal. I never will. I can't see myself devoting so much of my life to that goal. I am glad someone did. It shows me a path to a distant star that perhaps I can follow part of the way.

A couple of years later, a member of IHLRN who presents workshops in Chicago had the Lama Govinda and Fritz Perls spend the night at her home after they had finished their workshops.

Fritz Perls was the developer of an important field in psychotherapy called Gestalt Therapy. Fritz Perls was the ultimate egoist. The Lama Govinda was the ultimate non-egoist.

Fritz tried to dominate the evening and overwhelm the lama, impress him and be the centre of attention, but the ultimate egoist could not penetrate the ultimate non-egoist. Fritz Perls got up and tap danced in the middle of the living room.

The Treasure Hunter

I'VE ALWAYS WANTED to find buried treasure. It must be left over from my childhood fantasies.

I have made four or five trips to Alaska. It is wonderful to find a piece of our earth where nature is in control and man is the outsider. People are more democratic in Alaska. The bell boy in an Anchorage hotel treats you as an equal. People can still live off the land, growing vegetables, catching salmon, killing a moose – which gets them 2,500 pounds of meat. There may still be a lottery that any resident of one year or more in Alaska can enter. The state offers a parcel of land. If you win and build a house on the property within five years, it's yours.

Alaska is also a great place to pan for flecks of gold. Panning is hard work, but it was the only way for me to find at least one fleck of gold. I found nothing in my first four trips, but on the fifth trip … !

I was on the slopes of Mount Denali where some gold mining was still going on. I started my panning in a rushing mountain stream. Having no waterproof boots, I was forced to leap onto a rock in the middle of the stream, precariously keeping my balance while working the sands on the upstream side of the rock. Gold is heavy and tends to accumulate on the upstream side of rocks.

On my third panful, I spotted a shining object about a quarter of an inch wide and a half an inch long. No excitement. It was nice and shiny like gold, but mica, which has no value, can also look like a piece of gold.

The way to tell golden mica from real gold is to bend it. Mica is brittle and will crack.

I bent it. It didn't crack. It bent. It was a fleck of gold!

Excited, I picked the piece of gold out of the pan and bent it once more to confirm the find.

In my excitement I placed the gold in the palm of my hand and jerked my hand upward. The gold went flying up in the air and down the river.

I didn't keep it, but by God I'd found it.

My Dream Come True

MY TARZAN safari movie was about to happen with a hike into the remote Jimmy Valley of New Guinea. Dave, our guide, assembled twelve bearers, all muscles with strong shining black bodies.

Dreams rarely meet reality. Many of the bearers were proud of small bits of Western clothing. Some had socks with no shoes, so the bottoms wore out. Another few had accumulated t-shirts that were never washed and were full of holes.

Our great white guide started with a long and passionate speech to the bearers. Translation: "If your head bundles get too heavy, don't throw them into the jungle. I'll change the weight bearing."

In all our glory and in single file, we started walking down the jungle trail.

Halfway down, my wife sprained her ankle. Our great white guide carried her on his back for the rest of our trip to the first village, at least four or five miles. He hung back so the bearers couldn't see him. (If they saw him carry her, he would have lost face.) I walked ahead, watched the bearers so they wouldn't throw our goods into the jungle.

We made it to the first cannibal village. Waiting for us was a native hut built for the Australian patrol officers as they travelled between communities trying to stop killing and cannibalism. They carried no guns, only travelling with a large police dog, an animal unknown and frightening to the natives.

Treasure At Last!

I COLLECTED ten spectacular pieces of New Guinea art. I transported them from the upper reaches of the Sepik River in a huge dugout canoe decorated with an alligator prow.

Down river was a small settlement where a defrocked priest handled trade in New Guinea carvings. I gambled and paid him to ship them to me in America.

I waited one year, two years, three years. Nothing.

Through my connections in Australia I located a competent lawyer in Port Moresby, New Guinea's capital. He searched all over the island and six months later found my sculptures abandoned in a warehouse in the town of Wewack.

Eight months later, US Customs notified me that four hundred pounds of artifacts had arrived. The weight was too little, damn it. Customs wanted me to come to their headquarters to pick them up. I rented a truck and found ten crates carefully boxed in rare wood. Joy! They clearly weighed many thousands of pounds. I got my jungle treasures!

At my house I looked in the back of the truck. A great three-and-a-half-inch black beetle broke loose. In a panic, I squashed it with my foot.

Friends helped me carry the boxes to my barn, where I arranged for a champagne-led opening party that night.

It was joyous. Each box was crammed with thousands of tiny rolls of paper to protect its contents. My treasure was being revealed.

There were many dance masks, a giant alligator mask, a full body dance mask, a beautiful carawara hook. The carawara hook is a storage unit hung from the centre ceiling of a hut. It is a very abstract carving of the outline of a skeletal man. The ribs serves as handles for baskets of food so the rats can't get at them.

There was a giant ancestor figure about nine feet tall, naked and peeing on a chicken.

The largest box, about fifteen feet long and eighteen inches square, was the pièce de résistance – a lintel from a Haus Tambaran. The Haus Tambaran is the native religious structure, rising to a point four stories high. Over the entrance is the lintel, with about twenty ancestral spirit faces gracing its length.

Opening and removing the papers took a long time. This was not the lintel I collected! The one I collected was a masterpiece. The one I received was historically interesting but not an aesthetic masterpiece.

I was very upset. I had actually traded with the artist who had carved it. (It was possible for him to sell it to me because the particular Haus Tambaran had decayed and was being taken down, therefore, it was no longer sacred.)

Despite my disappointment, I took photos of all my artifacts to have them insured by a New York primitive art dealer. She found my lintel valuable. In fact, she declared that she herself had bought it when she was last in New Guinea, and had paid a chieftain for it by trading him a used truck. She was startled to see that it had been delivered to me, but made no claim to the carving. She understood it had wound up in my hands, and she knew nothing works as expected in New Guinea.

Years later I saw my missing masterpiece on a New Guinea stamp and found that it was housed in a museum in Port Moresby.

Harvey R. Wasserman

Max Taylor – The Mother Of All Battles

IN MY LOWER middle-class Jewish neighbourhood in the Bronx, New York, boys didn't fight except to get good grades at school that might produce nirvana – perhaps even medical school.

We lived at the high edge of a pleasant middle-class neighbourhood. At the bottom of the hill was a Jewish slum with gangsters, gangs and murderers. Money was tight during the Great Depression, so I was sent to a religious school at the bottom of the hill.

The other students in the religious Hebrew school hated me. I was polite, did my work and was a teacher's favourite. My schoolmates tried to beat me up after school every day. No chance. I became the fastest runner in the Bronx. I forged a note from my mother to let me out of class five minutes early. I left school on a dead run, five days a week, for three years.

At another time in my neighbourhood, a gang surrounded me at knife point. They relieved me of my weekly allowance of twenty-five cents.

My favourite "that's the way it was in the Bronx" memory happened at one side of Mount Eden Park. One side of the park bordered my neighbourhood. On another side it bordered the Bathgate Avenue slums at the bottom of the hill. A gang of boys moved in behind me as I walked along the edge of the park. When they got close, they shouted that they were going to get me, raised an axe in the air and promised to sink it into my skull. I had not the slightest doubt that they would. The thundering herd came running after me. I wasn't afraid. They were seventy-five feet away. I proved once more I was the fastest runner in the Bronx.

Move forward in time forty years. I am a professor at Yale University College of Medicine Department of Psychiatry. I sign up for a workshop with the Californian Esalen Institute, a radical experimental psychotherapy centre from the Big Sur coast of California. We were divided into groups of ten with a teacher named "Sookey."

My group included Dr. Max Taylor. At our first group together, Max started picking on me, insulting, criticising and diminishing me. I had done nothing to offend him. I waited for him to stop. He didn't stop. I politely asked him to stop. He didn't stop.

"Max, cut it out!" I demanded. He didn't stop.

Sookey intervened. "The two of you will have to fight. The fight will take place after lunch - it is lunchtime now."

Dr. Max Taylor became all the bullies I had ever run from. *NO MORE.* He was fifteen years younger, shorter but notice-ably muscular. I wasn't going to run. I would go down fighting. *NO MORE! NO FEAR!* I was recovering from the flu and still a bit weak. I knew he would win. *NO MORE!* I would give it my all. I would go down fighting.

The fight was arranged in a large room. All the furniture was removed. The room was encircled with people so that nei-ther of us could hit a hard solid object. The rules of the fight were simple. We were to hit each other only on the open palm of our opponent's hands and only with our open palm.

"Let the fight begin."

Max and I moved rapidly to the centre of the circle. Our palms encountered each other with a loud slap and an unpleas-ant stinging feeling. Max went flying. I stood stone still.

He's faking.

We came together again, palms slapping. Max went flying. I stood stone still.

Maybe he's not faking.

We met a third time. Max went flying. I stood still.

I can destroy this bastard!

As we met for fourth time, I met his right hand with my left. With no conscious plan, I withdrew my right hand. Max started to fall forward and to his left. I noticed my right heel start to leave the ground. I began to lift my right knee. I suddenly realised that I was on my way to remove his jaw. I immediately ended the fight and walked away.

One hour later, the amazing consequences of our battle became clear to me. I was at least three-quarters of an inch taller and incredibly powerful. I easily lifted my one hundred and forty-five pound wife over my head with one hand. I had become King Kong, Superman. What a reassuring discovery. I felt invincible to any attack - to any injustice.

The next day I found Max lying on top of group member Linda, dry raping her in the centre of the group. I had become fond of her. She had indirectly invited his revolting behaviour. I was going to rescue her, but only when Max the abuser had gone too far and Linda cried out for help.

I created my plan. I would ask the other men (those wimps) to help me get that bastard off her. If they did not respond, I would walk calmly and speak calmly to Max. "I will count to three. If you are not off her, I will break your arm." I knew I could do it, it was not a problem.

She called, "Help me." I asked the assembled wimps to help me get that bastard off her. Thank god they did.

The next day Sookey asked the group to take off their clothes. She really believed that the naked honesty of a nude group was more powerfully therapeutic. Everyone but one went naked. Can you guess who? Me. I refused, despite group pressure, to join them. They all thought I was too shy. Nuts. I didn't like some of the sexual innuendo in the group. I especially didn't like Max's salacious, vulgar comments to an older woman. *Let them think I am shy. Why bother to dissuade them?* I was there to learn and observe, not to take over or start another conflict.

On that last day of the five-day workshop, I overheard Max whisper to Sookey, "I will get the guys to go after Harvey and take his clothes off."

Can you guess my response? I will bet not. No one ever has.

John Wayne and the Fierce Kuga-Kugas

I lay on my back anticipating the attack with delight. If they ripped my clothes off against my will, that violation justified any response on my part. It didn't matter that it was nine against one, and the one was on his back. There would be blood and broken bones all over, none of them mine.

I was sorry to hear Sookey say, "No."

I was King Kong, Superman. I slowly returned to my old self. It only took six weeks.

Self-Esteem Eye Exercise

SELF-ESTEEM is the foundation of personality and is not to be confused with arrogance or perfection. It is simply liking and respecting yourself as you are, aware of your assets and weaknesses.

Here is an exercise to improve self-esteem. This one is short and simple.

Sit comfortably on a chair, speak out loud and say, "I love myself." Give it a truth number rating from one to ten, with ten being absolutely true and one the total opposite.

(a) Turn your head and eyes strongly up and to the left and imagine how you would look with perfect self-esteem. Hold this for thirty seconds.

(b) Turn your head and eyes strongly up and to the right. Imagine a video company learning of your improvement is filming a documentary about all the changes in you, walking, standing, talking and interacting with people. Visualise this for thirty seconds.

(c) Turn your head and eyes down and to the right. Imagine you are watching an edited version of the video made by the video company on a screen. Watch this for ten seconds. Then imagine walking up to the screen, stepping into the screen and becoming the person in the screen for thirty seconds. Return to normal and say again, "I love myself."

If your truth number score improved at least one-half to one point, do this exercise twice daily for six weeks.

Self-Esteem Body Exercise

ALL OF MY CAREER I've been searching for ways to help people with their self-esteem. Self-esteem is the foundation of personality. With good self-esteem, the difficulties of life are more easily mastered. With good self-esteem, your life dreams are much more likely to happen.

Basic self-esteem comes from the amount of unconditional love you received in your first three or four years. Relationships and events after that can increase or decrease your self-esteem, but the basic foundation has been sculpted into your consciousness.

I have found that positive affirmations are not very effective in improving this important state of mind. Please feel free to try the following:

Lie flat on your back on a mattress, knees bent and feet flat on the mattress.

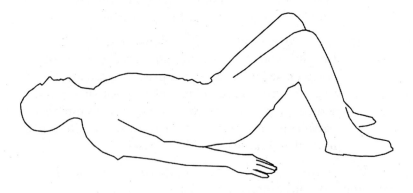

Say out loud, "I love myself."

Rate your reaction from 1 to 10, 1 equals not true, 10 is the ideal. You need a resonance level within yourself of 7.5 or better to have a decent quality of life.

Now rotate your pelvis downward into the mattress while inhaling.

Harvey R. Wasserman

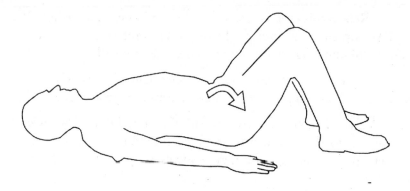

On exhaling, roll your pelvis upward, and roll your spine up, allowing your back to rise until you are resting at shoulder-blade level. Make certain you roll your spine up, don't do it stiffly. Don't jerk it up.

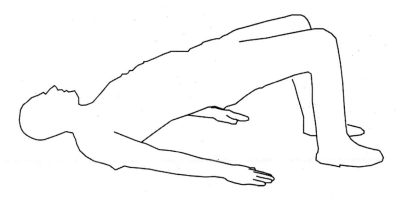

Now inhale and during the inhalation gently return your back to the mattress. Rotate your pelvis into the mattress.

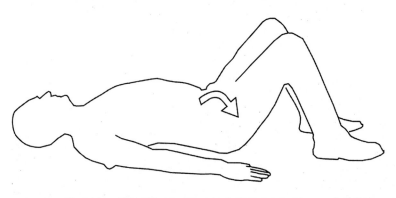

Repeat this exercise for about three minutes, then repeat, "I love myself," and rate it. Even a one-point increase in self-esteem immediately improves your sense of well-being.

Repeat this exercise once or twice daily for six weeks or longer. You will probably achieve a lasting improvement.

If you become anxious instead of feeling better, your welcome into this world was less than desirable. You probably need professional psychotherapeutic help.

Harvey R. Wasserman

Creativity

WE ALL HAVE vast amounts of belief systems that cover every small and large phenomenon in our lives. They are embroidered in our minds by our parents, family, friends and culture. For most of us these beliefs are our security system and we are uncomfortable when they are questioned. Try questioning Mohammed in a group of radical Muslims.

When Darwin's ship, *The Beagle*, anchored in a bay at the Tierra Del Fuego, which is at the tip of South America, the primitive natives had dugout canoes. They literally could not see the sailing ship.

In remote areas of Africa, when a plane comes in from a distance the natives believe that it is tiny and grows larger as it gets closer.

Creative people doodle asymmetrically, uncreative people doodle symmetrically.

When your beliefs fracture and are not yet replaced with a more eloquent belief, you are in the unformed place. You are not where you were, and you are not where you are going to be. In the unformed place there may be some excitement, but some anxiety is almost inevitable and must be tolerated.

If you are a creative person and that creativity is suppressed, the result is a flattening of a personality, even depression. Tom was a very intelligent and creative psychologist working for a government agency that was very conservative. The result was temporary psychosis until he broke free and went off on his own.

Jim loved writing music and was pressured to be an academic with a career and a pension. Finally tied down as a successful academic with children and a mortgage, he came to me depressed. With time he accepted his situation, felt and resolved his pain, and his depression was gone.

I am intermittently creative. If I stay constructive instead of creative for a long period of time, a good part of my joy retires from me. When I am creative in any form — painting, writing, new approaches in psychotherapy – it doesn't matter – joy is mine.

Cross-Country Trip

SATURDAY WE BOUGHT a pre-World War II car that had been sitting in a garage idle for four years. Sunday I started my first long distance drive across the United States with my friend, Otto.

We placed ads in the New York papers: "The war is over! We will sell your product across the United States." Plastics were a hot item, and we signed deals with a plastic tablecloth manufacturing company. Travel, adventure and hopefully sales and money would follow.

We hit the sales department of every store in every major city across the United States; Cleveland, Detroit, Chicago, Denver and many others.

For bachelor of science majors, we did well. I must admit Otto was a better salesman than I was.

Our car, which had slowly rotted during the war, provided the trip with adventure number one. A small town in Iowa approached at ninety miles per hour. Brakes were applied at the edge of town. No brakes – we flew through Main Street at ninety miles per hour playing high-speed dodge 'em right through the town. No hits, two near misses, no police cars.

Geared down to a stop at the exit of the town. Added brake fluid and the brake cylinders seemed to work well. Away we went.

Adventure two: stop at a gas station for fuel somewhere in Illinois. Gas attendant: "See that guy in the last car, he was a damn Jew. I can always spot them."

We two Jews listened quietly and lost the opportunity to correct a faulty recognition problem.

Adventure two (a): at a rodeo in some cowboy state, the master of ceremonies announces, "When we play "God Bless America," the audience cheers. When we play "There Is A Gold Mine In The Sky," the Jews stand up and salute." The audience laughs heartily. Am I really in my United States of America?

Adventure three: in a state campground, the heavens open up at midnight and our tent collapses. Otto and I strip naked and run around re-erecting our tent. In the morning we hear two ladies discussing their sighting of two naked men running around the camp the previous night, illuminated by lightning flashes.

Adventure four occurred in Yellowstone Park. To save gas, we hitchhiked around. At 8.30 in the morning, two cowboys in a sedan gave us a lift. This hospitable pair offered us a bottle of Southern Comfort whiskey. When we politely refused, they turned nasty. "Out here we tell if men are real men by the way they handle their whiskey." Otto and I had our first breakfast alcoholic drink. Now that we were certified real men, our hosts became genial once more.

Adventure five: our greatest adventure, mining in Burke, Idaho, is covered in Chapter Ten.

Our sixth and last adventure took place in the Olympic Mountains of Oregon. This adventure came closest to annihilating our human existence.

We were driving through the Olympic Mountains, heading down toward California. Uphill over the mountains was a breeze. But on our first steep descent, with Otto at the wheel, our brakes vanished.

Just ahead was a steep incline. We had to stop before the steep incline or we could only control our car by going off a cliff, a 2,000 foot drop, or smashing into the mountain wall.

Otto put the car into first gear when the brakes wouldn't hold. This didn't slow us down enough from what I could see, so I leaped out the running board, held onto the window frame and let my shoes drag on the road bed, providing I hoped a bit of friction to slow us down. Poor Otto thought I had abandoned ship, but between us we managed to stop within feet of the fatal descent. Otto was relieved to find my behaviour was heroic and that I hadn't abandoned him. Eventually the brake fluid got us to California, where with great relief we sold our car with its defects for a small profit.

Harvey R. Wasserman

They Are Only Sufis

TRAVELLING FROM the Aswan Egypt airport to the ancient temple of Luxor, our bus passed a parade of men dressed in white. They whirled as they moved forward, skirts billowing as they were whirling.

"What are they?"

"Only Sufis."

Only Sufis! The benevolent Muslim mystical whirling dervishes!

In the centre of the parade four men carried a sedan chair on their shoulders. The chair was completely shielded with white cloth.

"Probably a holy man."

As we were guided through the Luxor temple, the white parade arrived.

"I'm going with the Sufis."

"You can't," commanded our guide.

"The hell I can't!" I rolled under the barbed wire fence surrounding the Luxor temple.

I watched the whirling dancers. Several of their members played a trumpet-like instrument, setting pace for the whirling dancers.

Several Egyptian soldiers came to watch. A Sufi partnered me with an Egyptian soldier, gave each of us five-foot-long sticks and taught us an ancient fight dance. This was just after the six-day Egypt-Israeli war. We whirled to the trumpet's rhythm and clashed sticks.

This was not only an ancient Pharaonic fight dance but was a spiritual and communion dance in which we carefully hit each other's sticks and not each other. I couldn't speak to the soldier. His English, my Egyptian, were non-existent.

As we danced, a profound and warm level of intimacy developed between myself and the soldier. No words were needed. If I had been Israeli, a few weeks earlier we would have tried to kill each other.

Through ritual dance I had found my brother.

A small mosque was built into the Luxor ruins. The Sufis invited me to enter. Much time had elapsed. I was afraid of losing my group.

I said goodbye to the Sufis and to my brother and rolled back under the barbed wire fence.

CHAPTER SEVEN

HEALING

Healing

Healing

EARLY IN 1981, a thirty-year-old married female PhD psychologist came to see me with an unusual presenting complaint.

"I can't get pregnant."

Out of my mouth came a spontaneous unprofessional prediction.

"You'll be pregnant in nine months."

I was startled by my own prediction.

We had a uniquely intense and productive psychotherapy relationship. Nine months later, when she returned from a vacation with her husband in New Orleans I spontaneously announced, "You're pregnant" as she walked into my consulting room.

"No I'm not," she replied.

One week later, all the symptoms of pregnancy appeared.

We worked together during her pregnancy. Seven-and-a-half months later she came into my office with her big belly and a crutch under her right arm. Something had deteriorated in her back. Her gynaecologist put her on crutches. What a sad, pathetic sight. I felt deeply compassionate and totally helpless.

With her permission, I placed my hands on her clothes at the area of great pain. I closed my eyes, went into some form of altered consciousness and saw a bright white band of light at the top of my visual field that announced itself as the hem of God's robe.

Suddenly there was a blow as if a rubber hammer had impacted her back. This was accompanied by blinding red/orange lights in my visual field, which she also saw in her visual field. I had applied no pressure, only gentle touch.

Her pain vanished and she left my office carrying the crutches in her hand. She was delighted. I was terrified.

Harvey R. Wasserman

SOME WEEKS LATER, an Episcopal priest patient came for his appointment buried in deep flu. He could barely speak and was feverish. I felt compassionate and helpless.

I laid him down on a couch in my office, closed my eyes and gently placed my hands on each side of his head. In my upper visual field I saw once more the hem of God's robe. Within moments he felt the illness being lifted out through the top of his head. His temperature dropped to normal. His speech became normal. His body aches were gone. He was delighted. I was terrified.

AFTER A WEEKEND of meditation and chanting at a Siddha Foundation workshop (a guru-led group from India), I started my Monday practice feeling I had experienced an unusual weekend but that nothing of note had affected me.

At 11 am a PhD psychologist patient of whom I was fond came for his appointment, in exquisite emotional pain.

I felt helpless. Suddenly a column of love, divine love, came down from the Universe, passed through my chest at the back of my heart, entered my patient and returned to the Universe. His emotional pain vanished.

The stream of divine love continued for the rest of the day. Each patient that I worked with felt incredibly improved with little or no effort on my part. I also noticed that I couldn't find any fear anywhere in my imagination. I fantasised that I was like a huge wheel of cheese and fear was a tiny mouse that could nibble at me forever and make no impact.

That evening I became uncomfortable. "If this continues I won't know who I am." This is a reaction I have heard from patients as negative parts of their character begin to melt away. I tell them that they are about to find out who they truly are.

I know I started to destroy what was happening. Bits of it lasted a day or two. I buried it.

One patient, a wealthy, depressed, miserable real estate investor, felt peace and happiness for the first time in his adult life. This bliss vanished by his Thursday appointment. He was angry when I couldn't make it happen again.

Thirty years later I began imagining this column of divine love every morning on my way to my office. After two weeks some of the original miracle reappeared. Then I forgot the whole thing. Recent pledges to myself to repeat the imaging are made and promptly forgotten.

Grace had been granted to me. I turned it down. I refused to alter my constricted vision of reality.

IN 1981 A PSYCHOTHERAPIST came to me complaining of fatigue and jaundice. I knew it was a malignancy. Several weeks later a biopsy diagnosed a huge, untreatable abdominal malignancy. It was inoperable and unresponsive to chemotherapy.

He was only thirty-two and not ready to die. He started on a programme of excellent health care including an organic diet. We started a programme of five days per week psychotherapy designed exclusively to locate and eliminate any and all negative thinking and character traits.

His doctor had given him six months to live. It was a very aggressive tumour. Two months later, because his doctors couldn't stand doing nothing, he was given a brief course of chemotherapy despite its negative prognosis.

My patient never looked sick. He never seemed to deteriorate. Six months later, he felt and looked fine. His oncologist did a diagnostic visualisation of his cancer. IT WAS GONE. NO TRACE. My patient gave me credit for his miraculous cure.

His sperm count from chemotherapy was massively diminished and his sperm distorted. Contraception was not felt to be necessary.

Happy ending. His wife became pregnant. After nine months of worry, she gave birth to a beautiful, normal, healthy little girl.

CHAPTER EIGHT

SPEAK YOUR TRUTH

The "No" Cure Of Dyspareunia

DYSPAREUNIA is a fancy medical way of describing painful sex. Jane was a sufferer. She was particularly upset because it was interfering with her deeply committed relationship.

Years before, Jane surrendered her virginity to someone she did not want to have sex with. She said "Yes." The sex was very painful.

Asking Jane why she said yes when she did not want to be intimate was very revealing.

"I was raised as a true Christian, to please and help anybody and everybody who asked. So I said yes. That's what I do".

The problem with her current boyfriend wasn't sex, it was "no." Only her vagina was able to say that for her. "No" is the most important word in any language, the word of autonomy.

I played a game with her in which I forcefully asked her to do things for me that were absolutely outrageous. For example, I asked her to vacuum my office after the session. She was to respond with the strongest "no" possible. Jane's response was pathetic.

I taught her to do a two-year-old temper tantrum. Her performance wouldn't have scared away a mouse.

Bio-energetic analysis is a therapy that combines body work and psychoanalysis. There is a bio-energetic exercise in which the patient lies on their back, knees bent and held together. Then the knees are slowly opened and closed, moving the bent thigh and legs. The purpose is to tire out the inner thigh muscles. The inner thigh muscles are part of the sexual apparatus and will be tight and rigid if there is sexual inhibition. When this exercise tires these inner thigh muscles, they start to vibrate from fatigue. The legs, the pelvis and eventually the entire body, head and neck included, will start to vibrate gently and pleasantly. This only happens when sexuality is comfortable and free. With Jane, nothing at all happened!

Harvey R. Wasserman

I explained to her the importance of "no." When "no" is suppressed, any "yes" is a response of compliant slavery. I suggested that she say "no" to any erotic request from her partner and then decide to proceed if she really wanted to participate. Her partner was informed of the therapeutic game and willingly agreed to participate.

In all other situations, with any requests, she was to stall for time — "I will let you know later" — and then decide. Even if she returned with a reluctant yes, the attempt at autonomy was a step forward.

Two weeks passed before I saw her again. She entered my office happy and glowing – two weeks of passionate, pain-free sex.

She had also replied to requests by her employer to work beyond her work time with a gentle but positive "no." I was amazed at the speed and ease and thoroughness of her transformation.

"No" is established in children during the terrible twos. A strong early suppression is usually slow and difficult to erase. Was this a flight into health? A flight into health that might disintegrate?

Several weeks of checking, evaluating her sexual comfort and the availability of the "no" in her personality, confirmed a change.

Speak Your Truth

I HAD the pleasure of working with Fritz Perls, the founder of Gestalt psychotherapy, for five days shortly before he died.

The workshop took place in a student's home living room and was too small for the number of people. On late arrival, I couldn't fit into the living room so I sat on the floor adjacent to the living room door and hung my body around the door-jamb, partially blocking the entrance.

A late-term pregnant lady therapist was in the living room. Late-term pregnant ladies have to urinate frequently. To do so, she had to get by me. I was watching Fritz. She was large and unwieldy and bumped into the other side of the doorway. She announced her presence not by asking me to move but by cursing me viciously.

Inspired by Fritz's presence rather than my nicey-nice middle-class little boy, I surprised myself with, "Go fuck yourself, lady!"

Immediately, electricity started shooting through my body — my ears, my eyes, my jaw, my face, every part of my trunk, my arms and my legs – everywhere. It was as if I had tapped into some universal electrical force of incredible power that did not hurt. I was stunned. I didn't know what was happening. I waited and waited to see if it would last. I waited fifteen, twenty minutes; it continued. I waited for a half hour; it continued.

Finally there was an opportunity to work with Fritz. I went up and sat in Fritz's patient chair and told him my story. His only response, in his Austrian accent was, "You are trying to give up being so controlled – very difficult."

That was his total intervention.

Two weeks later I went to a different psychotherapy workshop. My mind was very preoccupied with the experience I had just been through. I couldn't concentrate on being with my family, so I took myself to Fudruckers, a giant hamburger chain.

At Fudruckers there are six cashiers. You stand in line until one of them is free. They take your money and your order and your first name. They give you a cup to self-serve your own drink. In my mental preoccupation, I saw the cashier wave me over. I went through the procedure with the cashier. Then I moved with my plastic cup to the self-serve drink section.

While I was pouring my diet cola, a young woman assaulted me viciously. "You thoughtless, selfish bastard! You sneaked in line ahead of me!" — plus other choice expressions I prefer to forget.

I hadn't done any such thing. But Fritz was one week dead. I apologised. I tried to explain that I saw the cashier wave me over to her register. The abuse continued. My apology continued.

I was depressed for two days.

Diamonds Are Forever

WHEN I BECAME ENGAGED to Rhoda, my first wife, I made it very clear that I did not believe in diamond rings. Diamonds are artificially price controlled by the De Beers diamond syndicate of London. Diamonds are not rare or valuable.

Rhoda, my mother, and my mother-in-law-to-be all knew this was important to me. They secretly went to the diamond district in New York to pick up a diamond ring.

Rhoda and I were travelling on the Long Island Railroad. Casually she brought out and presented me with her two-carat diamond ring.

I went into shock, said nothing and in that moment lost a piece of my soul. I pathetically announced when I recovered that I wouldn't pay for it. My mother did.

My Friend Arthur Miller

ARTHUR MILLER was Buddy Neubardt's cousin. Buddy was my friend and classmate at Syracuse Medical School.

Buddy never mentioned Arthur Miller or his relationship with Arthur until *Death of a Salesman* was produced on Broadway. The reviews were spectacular. Arthur Miller and *Death of a Salesman* were being compared to the works of Shakespeare.

Buddy started telling me about Arthur. Arthur's family thought that he would amount to nothing until those amazing reviews appeared in the paper.

I became interested in Arthur Miller. I wasn't interested in Arthur as a writer. I was interested in him because he courageously stood up to the House Un-American Activities Committee. Arthur was threatened with jail by this witch hunting Un-American committee. Almost everybody else succumbed.

Would I have been able to stand up to the pressure the way Arthur did? Would I have capitulated just as so many others did? How do you know whether you have the courage of your convictions? I have a hunch that I would have been one of the people who surrendered.

On a visit to New York City, Arthur was interviewed during the winter programme of the 92nd Street Y. I was hoping Buddy would be there and he could introduce me to Arthur. I went. Buddy wasn't there. I was very impressed by Arthur during the interview. He had a sense of humour, was warm, intelligent, humble and idealistic. "What a great friend he would make." I saw a man I would love to be friends with.

Later, *The London Times* reviewed one of Arthur's plays. The review mentioned that Arthur was having trouble with his back.

I wrote a letter to Arthur and told him I was doctor and a friend of his cousin Buddy Neubardt. I told him that I had a very unusual healing device that uses light for healing. The device is called the Lux IV. It was developed by a brilliant English inventor, Jon Whale. The Lux IV uses various forms of light to decrease inflammation and promote healing. I had had success treating several friends with severe back problems.

One week later there was an email from Arthur. He was very interested. Arthur gave me his phone numbers in New York City and in upstate New York.

I called Arthur a few days later. I lied to him. I told him that I had a family commitment in New York the first week in November. I didn't want Arthur to feel obligated. Arthur was enthusiastic.

The date was set for that Monday. The trip cost me about $5,000. I cancelled a week of appointments with my patients. There were airline tickets, hotels, indulgence in five Broadway shows. The Lux is easy to carry in a suitcase, but the lights that deliver the treatment are very heavy and require a special stand. For $1,000 I ordered a stand that I could transport unassembled in my airline luggage. Everything was arranged for me to work with Arthur.

Driving by taxi to his home in Manhattan, I was very nervous about hoping to make a friend. After being blackballed out of a medical fraternity, I labelled myself "Lone Wolf Wasserman." *I'll never make myself that vulnerable again.*

When I introduced myself to Arthur he was cold and aloof. He really didn't know what he was getting into. All previous attempts to heal him had failed, including serious back surgery. I imagined that Arthur was a liberal politically but conservative medically.

I treated Arthur's back. During the treatment he was cold, distant and unfriendly. When I finished with his back, he told me he had a serious problem with a broken bone in his ankle and asked me to treat it.

When I finished treating his ankle, Arthur said, "One thing I can tell you is I can't move my ankle without pain, and it is usually very hard to bend."

He pushed his foot over the edge of his bed and started to bend his ankle. His eyes got wide, his mouth slightly open. He was stunned. He couldn't believe that his ankle was moving without pain. He then got up and walked around with a mystified look on his face. "Well it's not hurting now," he said, referring to his back. He was amazed that his ankle and back were feeling better.

I left. No warmth, no real goodbyes. It had been an unpleasant, almost miserable experience. I certainly hadn't made a friend.

The second treatment was two days later. I arrived with as much anxiety as on the first day, not really looking forward to the experience of treating Arthur. Arthur was emotionally not there, but he submitted to treatment.

In the middle of the treatment I felt a drop in the temperature of the inflamed areas. There were other indicators that something very positive was happening.

One thing I did notice was that when I was aware of Arthur, I experienced him as a wall of integrity. This was something I never felt with another human being.

The goodbyes after the second treatment were half-hearted. I remember complaining to my wife that I didn't feel good about the whole experience of coming to New York. He was not hospitable in any way; he didn't even offer me a glass of water or a cup of coffee. I was feeling discouraged. I only went back the next day because it was the right thing to do. I had agreed to do it.

The next day Arthur welcomed me. There was warmth and a feeling of enormous trust. Everything was different. Arthur was warm and friendly. He responded to everything I said. After the second treatment, he had gone for a walk. Normally he could only walk for half a block without severe pain. For the first time in years, he was able to walk ten blocks without pain. What a difference that made.

Before the treatment we sat and chatted. I told Arthur my best story, my John Wayne story. I was so nervous that I told my story in an awkward way. I have told that story many times, and that was the only time it came out of my mouth awkwardly. The only thing worse than not getting what you want is getting what you want.

Everything had changed. Arthur was extremely relaxed during the last treatment. He even fell asleep. The atmosphere in the apartment was wonderful. There was a feeling that Arthur and I had bonded in some way. There were several signs that Arthur and I noticed that this third and last treatment was very positive.

As I was about to go, Arthur asked, "How much do I owe you for this?"

We had never discussed anything about money. I blurted out, "I didn't come here for the money."

"Is there anything I can do for you?"

I fell silent. I couldn't speak for almost a minute. One of the things that I am good at is speaking. I don't remember another time in my life when I felt speechless. When I was able to speak, I was too terrified to say what I wanted. I blurted out, "I have a manuscript that I would like to have published."

Arthur replied, "Well, send me a copy, and I will show it to my agent." I did and never heard any more about *Joshua and the Nine Animals*, a shamanic fairy tale.

I had chickened out! What I really wanted to say was, "I came here to treat you because you deserve to be treated. You are suffering. You made a contribution to the times I live in. I came here to treat you because I hoped that through the treatment we would find a way to be friends. I know you would be a great friend. So would I."

I feel sad that I didn't have the courage to make myself vulnerable, to say what my heart really wanted to say.

The Fierce Kuga-Kugas: Doing The Right Thing For The Wrong Reason

THE FIERCE KUGA-KUGAS have killed more white people than any tribe in the highlands of New Guinea. They are a tribe of pygmy headhunter cannibals.

I knew none of this when I decided to pay a visit. I was interested in their burial customs, putting the dead on an elevated bamboo platform. As the body liquefied in the equatorial heat, they bathed in the droppings and absorbed their ancestor's spirit.

I checked with the Australian authorities, who told me that a patrol officer would be in the village. I chartered a plane and landed just after dawn. The plane was to return for me in the late afternoon.

The patrol officer was not there. No one had died, so there were no burial customs to be seen.

I was alone. I wandered around the village. The men were warming themselves around an open fire. I entertained them with candy and fireworks sparklers, which produced a positive response. All seemed well.

The year before I had been in Africa. Wandering by an isolated lake, I saw a black swan. I didn't know they existed. I crawled on my belly to get close. I scared him. He flew off. A large black feather fell from his left wing and landed at my feet.

A gift from the gods! My magic black swan feather would protect me from danger. I wear it in my hat whenever I go into the wilderness. No harm has ever come to me.

In New Guinea, valued in decreasing importance were land, pigs, feathers, and females. Feathers were used for all ceremonies, including going into battle.

Walking on a trail at the edge of the village, I couldn't hear the barefoot little prick sneaking up behind me. He jumped up, grabbed my feather and ran.

I turned around. *That little bastard stole my magic black swan feather!*

I went after him, enraged. Twice his height and better fed, I ran him down in two city blocks. I anchored one hand on his shoulder and grabbed my magic black swan feather.

I stood in front of him, arrogantly took off my hat, arrogantly inserted the feather and arrogantly replaced the feathered hat on my head. With a look of contempt I turned and walked away.

On returning to an Australian enclave, I found out how dangerous the Kuga-Kugas were. First they will take a small thing from you. If there is no resistance, they will come for more and more and eventually kill you.

I did the right thing for the wrong reason. Or was it?

Harvey R. Wasserman

CHAPTER NINE

SPIRITUALITY AND MYSTICISM

The Divine Is In Your Belly

SHOUT vicious hatred out loud. Put all your venom into it. Then:

Take in six or seven deep, jerky in-breaths while tightening your belly muscles and pelvic floor (anus and/or vagina) in the same jerky manner.

Hold your breath in and keep the muscles tight for ten or fifteen seconds.

Then breathe out and relax and expand your pelvic floor and belly in the same jerky rhythm.

Once you have mastered this, repeat three times.

Now shout your negativity once more. You will find yourself unable to do so, or if you can, the venom will have vanished. Repeated regularly for six weeks, you may have a more permanent effect. You can also use this in a negativity emergency.

A Lion Next To My Bed

I WAS SIX years old, about to go to sleep. A full-grown, full-maned lion appeared next to my bed. He faced me. He was not threatening.

"Ma, there is a lion next to my bed."

"Harvey, go to sleep. You're just imagining it."

Five minutes later.

"Ma, the lion is still next to my bed."

My mother came into my bedroom. She turned on the light. The lion disappeared.

All during my life, this memory returns. Why is the lion still there? What does he have to tell me, to teach me? What part of the lion have I failed to make a part of me?

Today I will talk to my lion.

"Why do you keep coming?"

"Because you have not made me a full part of yourself. I am your power, your fearless power. I am still outside of you."

Demousing Plus Mystical Intervention

BILL, a protestant clergyman, was a powerful personality. He was used by his bishop to handle problems in the parishes. Maisie, his wife, was slender, sweet, passive and the spiritual one in the relationship. He dominated the relationship. She was cowed, afraid to speak up, reacting with emotional and sexual withdrawal, a quiet mouse.

In couples therapy, she had the courage to speak up. Twice I had to tackle him to prevent him from physically assaulting his wife. I decided that seeing them together wouldn't work. Maisie needed to be "demoused" so that she could stand up to his verbal and physical assaults.

You may be interested in what I call demousing. I have my patient teach me in great detail how they are verbally abused. I then tell them I want to play a therapeutic game with them. I will with all my acting skills play the part of their abuser. "I am only acting."

The patient is not to speak, but to move their consciousness slowly through their mind until they find a place where the abuse seems not to penetrate, even to bounce off them. As they do this, I can sense when they are close to that place. I tell them that they are close.

When they reach the exact location, I can no longer spew the abuse with any feeling and sometimes can't even get it out of my mouth. The place is usually near what I call the centre of consciousness, the place where thoughts seem to emerge. In most, but not all people, this is found in the middle of the skull, two and a half inches in front of the ear.

When this is achieved, I have them stay in that area for a few minutes while I continue to try and abuse them. Then I have the patient briefly return to their more normal, vulnerable consciousness, moving away from the area of self-respect. I encourage them to shuttle back and forth, spending four to five times the amount of time in the positive area.

When the demoused patient begins to interact with their mate, inevitably there is an initial attempt to get them to back down, to return to the way they were. When this fails, the partner sometimes changes and accepts the structure of equal power without domination. Sometimes the partner reacts with withdrawal, even abandoning the relationship. Therapists be warned, it is not unusual for the partner to stop paying for the therapy of the "mouse" that turned.

In this situation Maisie had difficulty responding to demousing.

Then a column of shimmering golden light two and half feet in diameter appeared in my office. The column was from floor to ceiling. I saw it. Maisie did not.

I instructed her to stand in the column of light. I would like to report a miraculous instantaneous change. Change did happen. Maisie began to respond to the demousing training. In a few weeks her passiveness with her husband became a thing of the past. After a brief initial resistance, Bill accepted the new relationship with Maisie. Communication, equality, replaced terrorism.

The Death Of Atheism

DO YOU RECALL the column of shimmering gold light in the previous section, Demousing Plus Mystical Intervention?

The patient's life was transformed by a column of shimmering gold light. What I failed to mention – SO WAS MY LIFE TRANSFORMED!

I was the only one who saw the column of shimmering gold light. Never had I seen a column of gold shimmering light in my office.

When I saw it, I immediately thought, *That's God's light.* Thought one, immediately followed by thought two. *If I had thought one, I am no longer an atheist. What am I?*

Atheism had been a core belief at my very centre. I became a card-carrying atheist at the age of six years. Science became everything.

Everything I saw about the religion that was around me was half-hearted, two-faced and even silly. One night I stood up on my bed in my pajamas, alone in my room at bedtime. I pointed at the heavens and called God every foul name that my six years had collected. At the very least I expected to be struck by lightning.

There was a deafening silence. Nothing happened! "You don't exist. You're a phoney."

At the age of 46, not knowing what I was, was very unsettling, a rupture in my belief system, my personality and my understanding of the universe. This emptiness and confusion lasted for weeks.

Then I was invited to a weekend workshop with a Kabbalistic rabbi. Kabbalism is a mystical form of Judaism that arose during the middle ages in the Middle East, probably Persia, probably an offshoot of Zoroastrianism.

Harvey R. Wasserman

On Shabbos, the holy Jewish Friday evening and sacred meal time for Jews, I enjoyed dinner with the rabbi and the other participants at the workshop. At the end of the meal the rabbi invited us to share any learning that had come to us during the week and to ask him any questions.

I told him my story. I told him that I didn't know what I was.

"Not a problem," he replied. "You're a seeker."

I knew he was right. I was now a seeker. What a relief to know who and what I was. A door had opened. Many experiences passed through that door, experiences that I have shared with only a few loving, trusted friends. Do I want now to share them with you? Yes I do. It is time.

Seeing The Light(s)

MY MOTHER died on Monday. Wednesday was her funeral. Saturday I was scheduled to be assistant trainer at a bioenergetic therapy workshop.

Bioenergetics is a field of psychotherapy that uses body structure and movement of a patient to understand their character and history. It is similar to the way tree rings can tell you the age of a tree and the amount of moisture-induced growth each year.

If a woman has well-developed, solid legs and a mature pelvis, with a slight, young girl's chest and small breasts, her father was warm and cuddly until she was 5 or 6. After that, he saw her as female and withdrew physical closeness and some emotional warmth. The young girl is shocked, doesn't understand and her chest area does not mature properly.

At the Saturday workshop, Karl, the chief instructor, put me on my back and massaged my upper chest muscles to release the sadness he saw trapped in me. I felt a tidal wave of sadness envelope me from my feet, covering my entire body. I went into a trance and thought I was in a bed with people all around me. It was the students worrying about me as I stopped breathing and started turning blue. Karl massaged some acupuncture points. I began to breathe and came to normal consciousness.

I was wiped out and could only sit against the wall and watch what was going on. Karl was working on Lou's chest. I saw red lights coming out of Lou's chest.

"There are red lights coming out of Lou's chest."

"Yes," said Karl in a matter of fact manner. He had seen auras in childhood and never stopped. Many children see auras but stop when their descriptions are frowned upon.

From that moment I started to see lights of different colours around my patients. I intuitively knew what they meant, such as dirty yellow meant fear and deep dark purple was pain, emotional pain.

A patient coming in late for group therapy entered behind me, and the room was filled with black and red light. I was terrified. I knew there was danger. The patient was in a murderous rage with a shotgun in his car. I convinced him to give it up. When I called Karl and told him about this, he said "Oh, the devil's rage."

In the community psychiatric hospital, my medical student class brought in a 35-year-old man, smartly dressed and looking as if he had not a care in the world. He also brought in with him the biggest, most intense fear aura (dirty yellow) I had ever seen. I let him settle in, and he shared a few superficial bits of information with me.

"You have been terrified all your life and you hide it from everybody."

He reacted as if I had hit him on the head and was dumbstruck. After six or seven minutes of deep silence, I asked him if he'd had enough.

"Yes."

After he was returned to his ward, the medical students wanted to know how I knew. I couldn't tell them. It would have ended my career at Yale, because Yale doesn't believe in auras. I desperately made up a fib and changed the focus of the class.

I see patients with medical student classes without any advance information so I can demonstrate how observation and interaction can reveal significant clinical information.

The patient for another medical class was a nice-looking young woman. I was enveloped in black light when she passed me by on the way to her seat, something I had never seen before. Unfortunately, I ignored it. After a mediocre interview, the students told me that she was a he who was being prepared for a sex change operation. I had even had a slight sexual reaction to her. Him.

Further research into this phenomenon revealed that sex change patients are quite troubled people and have the highest rate of murdering psychiatrists of any psychiatric diagnostic category.

You don't see auras? That's ok. Do you sense things about people and don't know where the information comes from? Everything and everybody has an electro-magnetic field around it that can be sensed, if not seen. With the passage of time, I rarely see auras any more, but my ability to sense has increased enormously.

Karl can tell me the colour of any aura I see with his eyes closed. These electro-magnetic fields are sometimes sensed and read out visually. With practice, they can also be sensed vividly.

Be careful about the rigidity of your beliefs. Study a bit of quantum physics and your sense of conventional reality changes. My favourite is the twin electron slit phenomenon where one electron copies the behaviour of the other with no detectible means of communication.

The Great Pyramid

I CAN ADD to the mystery of the Great Pyramid of Cheops. My wife and I were alone in the so-called King's Chamber for over an hour. Part of the mystery for us was, where was the endless stream of tourists?

It wasn't a very large room, lit by only one inadequate light bulb. Under a high ceiling was a stone sarcophagus with no lid. We decided to meditate. I went to lie down in the sarcophagus. Stepping in, I noticed about an inch of fluid on the bottom. It had to be urine.

Choosing instead to lean against the stone walls, I moved my hand. Lights came out of my fingers. With one finger I was able to write my name in light in the air and watch it slowly fade from left to right, from H to N.

Amazed, I produced several exact repetitions. My wife was also astonished that she produced the same phenomenon with her name.

Then I closed my eyes to meditate. Pictures flashed through my head of a condensed history of mankind and civilisation.

As we walked down the great stone staircase, so curiously alone, we were transfixed by the mystery of our experience.

Carrying The Cross

IN THE OLD CITY of Jerusalem is a site where Christ was burdened with carrying the cross.

From this holy site, a tour takes tourists down the Via Dolorosa ending at the Church of the Holy Sepulchre where Christ was buried. The tour stops at each station of the cross, where prayers are said. On the day of my visit there was a large crowd. They were very excited because leading the group on this day was a famous, well-loved bishop from Chicago. He was in charge of the pilgrimage.

A huge cross made of four-inch-square lumber was provided for him. The cross was very heavy. It took three tourists to carry it. The electricity of spiritual excitement filled the air. When one pilgrim became tired, another would volunteer to take their place.

I surrendered to the atmosphere. My mind was penetrated with one thought, *I should help carry the cross.*

But I am an atheistic Jew, and we don't carry the cross on the Via Dolorosa.

Finally I couldn't resist any longer.

A space became available and I took my place carrying one-third of the cross. I carried the cross for over half the Via Dolorosa. I never felt tired. I carried it to the Church of the Holy Sepulchre. Every step of the way I revelled in a joyous, spiritual expansion. I was in the middle of the pilgrimage, in the middle of a spiritual high.

I suddenly noticed an Arab pickpocket working the crowd. I signalled my wife. She had already spotted him. Oh well, there probably were pickpockets in Jesus's time also.

Before entering the church, I lowered the cross. On entering the church, far from feeling the holy atmosphere, something felt very wrong, very bad and very negative in this most holy place where Christ was buried and rose from the dead.

Harvey R. Wasserman

I discovered later that there was much fighting among Christian groups as to where they could take their place in the Church. I was told that it can get quite nasty. What a disappointment. This world is not heaven.

Virginia Mayo And Predicting The Near Future

VIRGINIA MAYO was a minor Hollywood dumb blonde. I saw one of her pictures, *I Wanted Wings*, three times. I wasn't interested in Virginia, but I was nutty about aeroplanes.

The Long Island Railroad travels from Manhattan to parts of Long Island with a major station in Jamaica, Queens. I met Virginia Mayo in the station. She was publicising her new picture, *The Girl from Jones Beach*. The Long Island Railroad was forcing monthly commuters to wear photo identification badges so they couldn't lend their passes to anyone else.

As publicity for her and the railroad, I took her picture as if she was a commuter. The honour fell to me because I was the railroad photographer at the Jamaica Station.

It was a simple operation. The stationary camera faced a pillar that served as a backdrop for the photograph. I photographed thousands of commuters. One commuter in every hundred faced the pillar, nose to the concrete and not the camera.

I knew they were going to do that before they did that. I don't know how I knew, but I knew.

Solution: "Please turn around and face the camera."

The mystery was never solved.

When The Soul Must Be Free

AIDAN HAD MADE two serious suicide attempts.

At 20, he jumped off a cliff but was unable to kill himself. He only succeeded in permanently imprisoning himself in a wheelchair. At 22, while on a lake side vacation with his parents, when they were temporarily inattentive he rolled his wheelchair off a pier. The chair sank, and he floated.

His uncle was a good friend of mine and had been very helpful to me. After the second suicide attempt, with local therapy going nowhere, his uncle asked me to work with Aidan. I didn't want to. I didn't want the stress of working with someone so desperately suicidal without the support and protection of a hospital. This was not possible. I could not say no to Aidan's uncle. I contacted his previous therapist, who described Aidan as having "a soul too big for his body. I couldn't do a thing with him."

Aidan was lively, lively with cynicism and sarcasm energised by his brilliant, aggressive intellect. There was no overt sign of depression. Aidan assaulted everything I offered him. I always responded gently or with laughter, and I complimented his brilliant attacks even as I offered my alternative views. My sole aim was to establish a working relationship with him.

After several months there were minimal signs of Aidan softening. In one session, he described the flow of his life. The content he shared was mostly insignificant, but as he reviewed his early childhood he temporarily became radiant and glowing. Describing the rest of his life as disillusioned, his glow faded. His skin grew darker, a strange shading of grey.

I immediately concluded that he came into this world a uniquely spiritual, idealistic child. I asked him to imagine a column of shimmering gold light, from floor to ceiling, surrounding him in his wheelchair. The beautiful gold and shimmering light was to penetrate every tissue, cell, space and organ of his body.

The effect was immediate and dramatic. Aidan transformed into a warm, intelligent, responsive human being. Repeating the visualisation for several weeks was all that was needed. He returned to university with enthusiasm and graduated with honours, complete with a good professional job and a girlfriend. An eight-year follow-up via his uncle confirmed the quality of his transformation.

Aidan, born an enormously spiritual, idealistic child, suppressed his spiritual values as he encountered his world. The result was depression, despair and a major warping of his character. Miraculously, a single and often potent spiritual image returned him to who he was born to be.

"You Have No Soul"

"I FEEL EMBARRASSED saying this to you, but I keep having the thought that you have no soul."

She replied, without emotion, "That's what Dr. Blakestone who referred me to you said."

Deirdre, a 25-year-old depressed heroin addict, was now my patient. All I could think of was, "You have no soul." I didn't even know what a soul was. I probably never thought about a "soul" before. I also knew that I did not want to be any closer to her physically than I had to be.

Then! Oh my God! The smell of SULPHUR filled my office! It was as if someone had struck a match. There was no way a source of sulphur could have entered or originated in my office.

I was frightened. I immediately made the sign of the cross with my fingers. I am Jewish, but there is no way in hell or in an emergency to make the Star of David with your fingers. No wonder Christianity has more disciples than Judaism.

In thought, agitated and angry thought, I demanded that whatever was there leave in the name of every deity I could think of: God, Abraham, Moses, Jesus, Allah, Buddha, The Great Spirit.

The smell disappeared, and I felt more comfortable working with my "patient." A little useful patient-therapist exchange passed between us, but its memory has faded away against the background of the greater event that I was experiencing.

When the appointment time was up, I let her leave without making another appointment. I was too terrified of being in a situation that was beyond me. I never heard from her again.

One of my teachers knew a lot about unusual reality. I called him. "You did the right thing. You were angry at its presence and called on a higher power to help you."

He suggested that I put coarse sea salt in every corner of my office. "Negative entities can't enter a room radiating the energy of coarse sea salt." When I moved offices, I was startled to find small piles of sea salt in every corner.

My negative entity consultant also suggested I have a clergyman re-sanctify my office as a place of healing. At the time I was studying bioenergetic analysis, a neo-Reichian body-oriented therapy. One of my fellow students, an Episcopal priest, asked to come into treatment with me and as part of his therapy to do body work in the nude to better observe body movement and structure.

I asked him to make my office holy again. He agreed. "Get me a new crystal bowl, a palm leaf and water that I can bless and make holy." At the next appointment he prayed over the water, poured the holy water into the pure crystal bowl, dipped the palm frond in the holy water and sprayed the water as he visited every part of my office and uttered Latin prayers.

I began to laugh. "Do you realise you are doing a nude re-consecration?"

In laughter he replied, "In the history of the church, I am certain it's not the first time!"

Interpersonal Poisoning And Interpersonal Cure

THE TEACHER of Mariel Therapy was described to me as powerful, almost miraculous as a therapist. I attended her workshop.

After I observed her work, I told her that I could do and understand her approach, but she was much swifter than I was. "Can you help me become as quick as you are?"

She made an irrelevant remark about my father; that's all. A friend attending the workshop noticed that she didn't like my particular request for help.

The next day I woke up in a severe depression unlike any I had ever experienced. Nothing helped, not exercise or meditation or anything. It felt like someone else's depression was injected into me.

What could I do? I called Eleanor. Eleanor was a psychic healer that I had studied with. I described my dilemma.

"It's not your depression," replied Eleanor. "I will send you the fireball."

In my visual fields appeared an overwhelming burst of red and orange. The depression was gone.

What's Your Name?

POLARITY THERAPY is designed to balance the energy in your body. The therapist simultaneously touches specific points on your body with her right and left hand. It seemed to be helping me.

During my fifth session, while my eyes were closed, a small angel appeared on my forehead just above the space between my eyebrows, entered my body and grew to full size.

The front third of the angel was one with the back third of my body. Peace and harmony.

My next patient was in deep agony. Her beloved father was dying. In thought I asked the angel to comfort her. Enfolded in its wings, she relaxed, turned pink. There was surprise in her voice as she announced how much better she felt. Later that week she returned in agony. Again grace was granted.

One night in bed with my wife I asked my angel to comfort her. She knew nothing of my experience. "I am comforted," she whispered. I told her what was going on.

The angel was with me for three days and helped with many patients. Then it vanished.

Two weeks later, something frightened me. My angel suddenly appeared, comforted me, then vanished, never to reappear despite my many requests.

I am told I should have asked the angel its name. I didn't know that. My angel is still nameless to me.

I do know that angels do not have wings. What would they need wings for? They don't fly through the air. When they take human form, the energy of pure and unconditional love radiates out of each shoulder. Someone must have thought that they were wings.

Harvey R. Wasserman

Pray For God's Favour

A MESA is a long, narrow, flat mountain. First Mesa in the Arizona desert supports the oldest continuously occupied settlement in North America, home of the Hopi Indians.

My family and I were the last white people allowed to attend the sacred rattlesnake dance.

On approaching the village the sound of great drums beating filled the atmosphere and transformed time from the present to another, timeless, reality.

The snake clan had been collecting large rattlesnakes in the desert. For two weeks in sacred isolation they had been engaged in exercises with the rattlesnakes in their kiva (church), forbidden to any but the initiated.

When we arrived at the village square, the snake clan, elaborately painted and feathered, were dancing around in a large circle, each with a huge rattlesnake held in their teeth. Dancing backward with each snake dancer was a member of the deer clan. They were less elaborately painted and feathered. Each deer clan member waved a feather object in front of the snake's face and beat a small drum close to the reptile.

After one hour the dancing stopped. The snake clan members moved to the centre of the circle and created a pile of writhing rattlesnakes. The snake clan dancers left. Four men, each naked except for a brief loin cloth, ran into the pile of rattlesnakes. Each man lifted handfuls of snakes. With handfuls of snakes, one ran north, one ran south, one ran east, one ran west. They freed the rattlesnakes at the edge of the Mesa. The snakes carry messages to the gods, "Bring rain for the crops."

We were the last outsiders to be allowed to attend the ceremony. Recently I heard that due to lack of snake clan culture trainees, the ceremony was terminated. I had been privileged to enter another world. I feel sad the door to that world is now closed.

Native Intuitions (Micturition)

IT HAS BEEN SAID that when we gave up the primitive tribal life of our ancestors, we buried a good part of human intuition.

The cannibal chief of a village in the Jimmy Valley of New Guinea was living proof of this speculation. We lived in a patrol officer's hut at the edge of and out of sight of the village. Our toilet was a hole in the ground with bamboo poles transformed into a shield for privacy.

Every time my wife had to pee, the chief of the tribe appeared and followed her to the loo. I could go pee unmolested. The first time she was followed, she was terrified, and she fled back to me.

We devised a strategy. I would politely intercept and divert him with conversation, candy and cigarettes until she finished her business. It worked. When she returned to the hut, he went back to the village.

He appeared whenever she had to pee, midnight, two in the morning, 5 am, during the day. It did not matter. He had no way of directly observing us. He just knew. The cadences of this strange, peculiar and polite dance were repeated each time.

What did he want? He didn't seem aggressive. My final hypothesis was that he was curious to compare white women's versus black women's genitals.

Jewish Spirituality

I AM a cultural Jew. I am proud of my ancestral heritage.

Most of what I saw of religion as a kid made no sense to me or was hypocritical and superficial. That's why I became an atheist at the age of six, standing on my bed cursing God with pointed finger.

I wasn't struck by lightning! I shouted, "You're a phony. You don't exist!"

I made two failed attempts to make contact with organised religious Judaism as an adult.

When I established my practice in the US, I made contact with the local synagogue. I thought it would be good for my practice and wanted my kids to learn about their ancestral heritage.

The synagogue sent the head of their membership committee to my house. I was ready to hand him a cheque. But he made a mistake. He told me that when the synagogue needed a new roof, a meeting was called in the synagogue. The exit doors were locked.

"No one leaves until we have the money for the roof."

I know what I would have done: "Open the door and let me out or I'll break it down."

I didn't join.

Thinking of moving to Ireland, I contacted Ireland's Chief Rabbi, who invited me to services.

I got dressed up in a suit, tie, white shirt, shiny leather shoes and drove to Terenure, where the synagogue was located. My map showed two synagogues. Which was the one that belonged to the Chief Rabbi?

In my rented car on an early Saturday morning, I spotted a father and son all dressed up with formal hat wear. The son was pale like a young Jewish scholar should be. I followed them up an alley.

Suddenly the father turned and confronted me. "What are you doing here?"

"I came to pray."

"Get out of here! You are an abomination. You are not welcome here."

In his rage he turned red and looked like he wanted to kill us. My wife was shocked and started to cry. Oh my God, there are ultra conservative idiot Jews in Ireland! No wonder he was upset. I wasn't supposed to drive on Saturday, I was supposed to walk.

I hoped that the Chief Rabbi was in the other synagogue. I hid my car and walked.

We were welcomed. The service was three hours long. The focus of the Bible reading was how Solomon financed his temple. I was spiritually elevated as high as a crushed worm. I left. This was the end of my Irish Jewish experience.

Oh yes — I drove by the alleyway that led to the first synagogue. I fantasised buying a small pig and throwing it through the synagogue window.

Harvey R. Wasserman

Following Contact With The Ultra Orthodox Jews Of Ireland

LEAVING THE JEWS of Terenure behind, I drove into central Dublin for a little shopping therapy. It was Saturday. Parking was non-existent, but suddenly I saw an empty space. A delivery truck beat me to it. I waited, hoping it would be a quick delivery.

After a while I decided to go in to the merchant and find out if the delivery truck would be leaving soon. As I approached the shoe store, standing in front of it was a middle-aged, scruffily dressed man playing an accordion. He looked at me and put down his instrument. In a rage he shouted, "People who don't work, don't deserve to live!" He lunged at me.

I fled to my car and took off – screaming, "The Jews and the schizophrenics of Ireland are out to get me today!"

I was still angry at the ultra orthodox experience that I had with the Jewish community.

Schizophrenics are super sensitive to peoples' emotions, especially hostile ones.

The next day I was over my anger and walked by the accordion player. He ignored me and just kept on playing.

Feeling Up The Mother Superior

"GROUP THERAPY is the coming thing. I want you to become an expert. There is a two-week training session in New Hampshire this summer. Go for it."

Thus commanded Lou, my Department Chairman, to Harvey, Director of Education and Training.

Training started with group exercises in a private school gym. The fourth exercise was, "Pair up with someone you don't know." I had never met a Catholic nun. This was immediately after Vatican II. The church had opened up, with priests and nuns reaching out into the world. Several attended this group therapy training session. I picked a nun in full regalia.

"Sit back to back and explore each other's bodies," was the instruction. It's very hard to control where your hands go following these instructions. I could feel my partner's back stiffen and massive tension flow through it.

"Do you want to stop?"

"Yes."

"Do you want to get out of here?"

"Yes."

We left. She remained tense until she discovered my wife was part of the workshop. I had felt up and been explored by the Mother Superior of a cloistered order on her first experience out in the world. The next day she went out of her way to meet and make friends with my wife. We shared a lovely friendship for the remaining two weeks.

The Voice

DOROTHY was a most difficult patient. Traumatised by a divorce she didn't want, she specialised in hysteria, manipulation and intense sexual projection. She seduced a different man every night, rejected him in the morning. She was on a focussed search project to find the right man.

Her sexual intensity was present in my office. For the life of me, I couldn't figure out how she did it. It wasn't in her body movements, her voice or facial expression. Could it be that she was able to directly project sexual energy? I could explain it no other way. She also demanded to be special, admired, indulged, the centre of attention.

Keeping in control of the process of therapy was a major problem in working with Dorothy.

One day I lost it. She was in complete control of the session. I knew I had lost it. I felt lousy when she left.

I had a free hour after our session. I flooded myself with verbal abuse. I walked down my office stairs to bury my angst in a cup of coffee.

Halfway down the stairs, I heard a voice. It was a male voice of unconditional love. I couldn't tell if the voice was inside or outside of my head. "Have faith in yourself, my son."

I immediately felt wonderful. My sense of well-being lasted the entire day. Why has that voice never returned?

Six months later, a new patient started her first session with, "If I tell you what I have experienced, you'll think I'm crazy."

After much procrastination, she confessed to hearing a voice of unconditional love, a male voice saying, "All will be well. Respect and love yourself."

I knew it was the same voice I had heard. I added, "My voice was also a male voice of unconditional love. I, too, have heard it. If you're crazy, so am I."

This produced instant trust and communion between us. We rapidly moved on to personality and life issues that were marring her life.

A few years later, in the movie *Field of Dreams*, I heard the voice again. "If you build it, they will come," it said. It was the same voice, the same tone, the same unconditional love. This was a Hollywood movie. What the hell is going on?

Chakra Chant

YOU DON'T BELIEVE in chakras? At one time, neither did I. Chakras are believed to be areas of interaction at specific points on the body with some form of universal cosmic energy. Chakra energy is the ancient Hindu equivalent of Chinese chi energy.

I'm going to share a chakra chant stimulation. Try it and see if you feel better, stronger, more integrated. Most people do.

1. At the base of your spine, feel the sound created by making the sound of the letters H and L together. Start with the H sound and let it flow into the L sound. Repeat three times.

2. At a point just above your pelvic bone in the middle of your body, feel the effect of the sound of the letters VU. Pronounce the V first and then the U. Let them flow into each other. Repeat three times.

3. One and a half inches below your belly button, chant the sound of the letters RUNG. The sound will seem to be moving down from that point. Repeat three times.

4. Two and a half inches above your belly button, chant the sound made by pronouncing the letters RANG. The sound will feel like it is moving upwards. Repeat three times as with each of these chakra sounds.

5. In the middle of your breast bone, about three inches above the bottom of the breast bone, chant the sound made by pronouncing the letters YAM.

6. Just below your Adam's apple, sound of the letter A.

7. Between your eyebrows and up about a half inch, sound the chant of the letter E.

8. Chant the sound of the letter E and raise it in pitch until the sound disappears, but keep making the

sound. Hold this breath sound for a few seconds after the sound disappears. It should feel as if it is moving out and up from the centre top of your skull. Three times, lower the sound into the audible range, then elevate it to the inaudible range, the sound beyond sound.

Repeating this chakra chant regularly one or two times a day will produce a positive change in consciousness and a sense of well-being. Repeat regularly for at least six weeks for a persistent effect.

The Spiritualist Church

THE SPIRITUALIST CHURCH practices conventional Christian ritual and beliefs with a major exception, they believe their clergy can communicate with the departed. They do this at the end of every Sunday sermon. Sir Arthur Conan Doyle was a firm believer in the Spiritualist Church.

I had known for many years there was a Spiritualist Church in nearby Greenwich Connecticut.

One Sunday I decided to attend and see what it was like. I arrived early and sat in the front row and put up with the Church service. When it was Spiritualist time, I sat up very, very straight, hoping I would be selected. I was selected.

The female minister was performing the Spiritualist work that day. She had never met me. She made the following comments from the other world. "They are very interested in your use of music in your work." At that time I knew of no one else who used music as part of psychotherapy.

In a scolding tone, she reported, "Get on with your writing." I had bogged down on writing – I had totally stopped.

"A new woman has entered your life and will change it." I knew who she was, and I was terrified.

"A bridge is being built and will be completed in September." On September 30th, I realised this new woman loved me unconditionally like my grandma had. I knew that I loved her also. I divorced my schizophrenic wife and married the woman who has changed my life.

CHAPTER TEN

INDEPENDENCE, LEARNING, MAKING MISTAKES

Sometimes My Superiors Are Right
The Chance Of A Lifetime
And Sometimes My Superiors Are Wrong
Never Fly Ethiopian Airlines
The Payback Ceremony
The Corruption Of The Natives
Return To Civilization
Burke, Idaho
Attacked In Africa
Trip To Igasu Falls
The Fatal Lie

Sometimes My Superiors Are Right

"NEVER CHALLENGE a patient's delusions or paranoia" was my supervisor's advice when I started my psychiatric training. "They just get more upset."

I don't always follow the advice I am given. Sometimes I am right, and sometimes I am wrong.

George, a gentle patient on a locked psychiatric ward, announced, "I am the king of nature. If I change my arm position, thousands of babies' heads will be crushed. If I change my leg position, innumerable Catholics will die." For long periods he stood still as a statue.

I invited him for a chat in my office. I planned to inform him that he was not king of nature.

He mentioned his royal status once, and I told him that I did not believe he was king of nature. He ignored me. After a second confrontation, he ignored me. A third confrontation: "If I turn myself into a tiger here and now, will you believe I am king of nature?" I had to agree. "Of course, if I turn myself into a tiger, I am not responsible for the consequences."

As his demeanour changed from benign to belligerent, I immediately changed the subject. My supervisor was right.

Harvey R. Wasserman

The Chance Of A Lifetime

DR. HUGH GALBRAITH was the most remarkable mental healer it ever was my privilege to learn from. It only took Hugh five minutes to contact the human core of any patient, no matter how closed or how crazy. He was a legend at the Menninger School of Psychiatry.

Hugh once told me about a female patient in a jump suit. She suddenly stood up and zipped down, stark naked.

"You have a lovely body," replied Hugh. "Why did you want to show it to me?"

What sophistication. What therapeutic cool. Her response, not his, became the focus of therapeutic intervention.

I remembered that response and waited twenty years for the opportunity to use it.

Mary was a tall, well-built, 24-year-old girl. Her pleasant but undistinguished face was set off by the sexual fire storm she radiated from every cell in her body. Her father raised her to believe that her only asset as a female was sex.

A fashion designer patient who passed her in the hall described her. "She dresses like a hooker."

Mary told me that a Maserati sports car stopped next to her on Fifth Avenue in New York. The occupant offered her $50,000 to become his mistress.

On one memorable Thursday she came dressed in a military-style jump suit, stood up, zipped down stark naked, ready for my twenty-year-old response.

I couldn't utter a sound. I could only hold tightly to my chair.

Our silent encounter of one point five minutes ended. She zipped up, sat down and our psychotherapy continued as before. We both knew I passed the "Will you respond to me as a sexual object?" test.

Indeed I had passed the test, but not gracefully.

And Sometimes My Superiors Are Wrong

I DIDN'T LISTEN, and I saved a soul.

In my second year of training at the Menninger School of Psychiatry, I was assigned half time to a boys' reform school. My job was to do a psychological work-up of new admissions and present it at staff conference, where treatment decisions were made.

"DO NOT TRY TO DO TREATMENT. THEY ARE TOO DIFFICULT FOR YOUR LEVEL OF TRAINING."

On my third trip to the area where newcomers were kept, one boy who was not assigned to me launched an unprovoked vicious verbal attack against me. I was thrilled! He was just the kind of delinquent kid that the Austrian psychoanalyst August Aichhorn writes about. The next week he was assigned to me. I started treatment immediately. He attacked me immediately.

"That's a good attack," I replied, "but I am sure you can do better."

He looked stunned, mute and subdued. He accompanied me to my office. We had an agreeable and professional conversation.

He was brought to the Boys' Industrial School from a mental hospital. His serious crimes were breaking into the homes of wealthy people and shitting on their Persian rugs. Diagnosis was not crazy, but very angry, and so we met. Secretly I arranged to see him twice a week, always looking for an empty office.

"The jerk who runs this place just got a new sports car. I'm going to scratch the paint with a nail."

"I know him; he loves that car. If you really want to get him pissed off, pour sugar in his gas tank. It will destroy the engine."

"Do you want to get me sent to the pen?"

Aichhorn had developed a technique for establishing a close relationship with such boys. On the fourth week of visits, we sneaked into an empty office that contained a pool cue. Using the cue as a bat and my head as a ball, he swung and stopped just short of my head. I didn't flinch. This was the beginning! The following week no one was in the staff lounge. There was a pool table and coffee-making equipment.

"You take the coffee. I'll nick the sugar."

"What kind of petty idiot do you think I am to risk my medical reputation for a crummy can of coffee? A half a million would make more sense."

He didn't take the sugar.

One day when he knew in advance which office we were to use, he sneaked in early and unscrewed the bolt that controlled the tilt of the executive desk chair. We walked into the office together. He forgot! He sat on the chair! He tilted over!

Our contacts, with occasional mild relapses, became softer to occasionally mildly testing.

Guido came from a petty crime family where there was no love. I came from the Menninger School of Psychiatry, which was totally psychoanalytic and medically oriented. Finding Aichhorn's book was a miracle that would have been frowned upon. I knew Aichhorn had learned a way to make a healing intimate relationship with very delinquent boys: act smart, non-judgemental, fast, tough and in command. Think like a criminal (what fun that was!) but always point out the stupidity of that behaviour.

Aichhorn warned that as you succeed, watch for the sudden emerging of a sweet, needy little boy. You must immediately respond as caring friend or father. That's essential. Do not miss this!

Guido became an eight-year-old sweet boy. "I collect match book covers. Do you have any match book covers?"

"I don't, but I can get some."

I collected every match book cover I could find. The testing atrophied. Meetings became a sweet boy meeting intimately with a sweet adult male who happened to be professional.

All this took place over five months. It was time for my training to move on. Two weeks before I left, I told him I was being transferred. There was a BoBo in the room, a toy permitting aggressive discharge. Guido attacked it for twenty minutes and emerged sweet and emotionally close with me.

I never saw him again after our last session. I went back later and talked to the staff. They told me that about two-thirds of the way through our time together, he had made a positive relationship with the staff member who supervised his dormitory. They had seen a remarkable change in him that persisted after I left.

A soul had been saved!

Never Fly Ethiopian Airlines

ETHIOPIAN AIRLINES was the only carrier to have vacancies on flights from Kenya to Rome with a stopover in the city of Axum, where the ark of the covenant may be kept.

Two-thirds of the way to Axum, while flying way above high mountains, the breathing masks dropped. There was no oxygen in them. Our hostess assured us everything was fine. Lie. I am a licensed pilot. When my ears popped I knew the plane had lost its pressure. The air coming into the cabin would be low in oxygen.

Soon I felt lightheaded. Children passed out. Children and older people need higher levels of oxygen to maintain consciousness.

I had acquired a Masai spear, which was stored in the checked luggage. My Masai sword, however, was in my hand luggage. (There had been no security check-in.)

Did the pilots have their own oxygen system? Were we on auto-pilot with the pilots at least partially incapacitated? I could take out my sword and demand they fly lower. But what if the pilots were unconscious and couldn't land the plane? What should I do? What was the right decision?

At the point where I knew I had to decide, our plane started to descend.

Landing at Axum airport, we did not taxi to the terminal. After a pause, they rolled out a red carpet from the terminal to the plane. Haile Selassie, the Lion of Judah, The Emperor of Ethiopia, accompanied by an honour guard, came out to our plane to honour the President of Botswana. We did not know he had been travelling on our plane.

When I tell Rastafarians that I saw Haile Selassie, whom they worship as a god, they kiss my feet.

On to Rome, where customs took charge of my spear. "You can't take a spear into Rome."

"Are you really afraid I will spear somebody in Rome?"

"Those are the rules."

I bought *Time* magazine's hijacking special as I entered my hotel. Included was an article on how different countries treated captured hijackers. Under Ethiopian Airlines – every plane has two plainclothes police officers. They capture the terrorist, put a towel around his neck and cut his throat on the plane!

The Payback Ceremony

WHEN I VISITED New Guinea in 1971, large portions of it still were wild. At that time new tribes were still being identified by the Australian Government. Every day was filled with adventures, many of which you just had to be lucky to stumble upon. Such an adventure was the payback ceremony.

Payback ceremonies occurred every ten years when two tribes had decided to make peace. One time one tribe would give gifts to the other, and then it was reversed during the next payback ceremony.

The adventure took place on a huge grassy field. Alongside the field were many very long tables that had been constructed out of bamboo. At the end and barely visible in each field, the warriors of each tribe assembled, fully feathered and painted and carrying spears.

Suddenly martial drums from behind one group of warriors began to beat. The warriors started to move forward slowly and then on a dead run, with murderous cries, their spears held at the ready, they charged the other group, which remained stationary.

They charged two-thirds of the way to the other group, stopped, and with a different drum rhythm, marched back to where they started.

Then it was time for the other tribal warriors to do the same thing. Each side did this three times.

The most memorable charge of all was when the group charging from my right reached the position in the middle of the field near where I was standing. One of the warriors broke from the formation, charged in my direction, spear at the ready, looking ferocious, stopped in front of me, smiled and shook my hand. It was an interesting but startling experience.

After the charges were finished, gifts were put on all the tables. One at a time each warrior held up his gift and made a long speech and presented it to the other side. We watched this for about forty-five minutes or an hour. We could tell it was going to go on for many, many hours. At that point we left.

Harvey R. Wasserman

The Corruption Of The Natives

AN AMAZING SIGHT appeared as we drove through the rough New Guinea jungle and came to a clearing.

A hundred and fifty natives, a few in full war paint and feathers, were lined up in a semicircle. At the apex of the circle was a Land Rover, its open back doors facing the semicircle. At the Land Rover were a white man and a native in Western clothing.

The native reached into a box and gave each warrior a small package. Then he shouted, "Hormel ham!" Raising their prize high in the air, they explosively chanted, "Hormel ham! Hormel ham!"

The native helper dipped a ladle into a large milk can after distributing paper cups to the warriors. He carefully filled each cup with liquid, then shouted, "Ovaltine!" The war cry, "Ovaltine!" rang out three times.

With "Social Tea Biscuits!" ringing in our ears, awe struck, we drove away.

We had seen the indoctrination of a hunter-gatherer and farming people into consumerism.

They would soon be taught to grow coffee for money and educated about money and purchasing. Small log stores would be scattered through the jungle. The natives were very brand loyal.

Return To Civilisation

AFTER TEN DAYS of exploring the Jimmy Valley, it was a long, steep and exhausting hike out.

We left at dawn. After many short stops to rest and chew sugar cane, we reached a grass field where a light plane awaited us.

The pilot wanted payment before he flew. "I can't accept your American dollars."

"Why not?" I was in shock and penniless in the middle of the New Guinea wilderness.

"I don't know what the problem is. I got a cable from Australia saying don't accept US dollars."

My impoverished panic was relieved by a loan from our guide. What had happened, nuclear war? What else? I didn't know.

On arriving in civilisation, we found that Nixon had devalued the American dollar, and its worth had not yet been established.

Thank God for our American Express card, which paid in local currency. We were ok again. I never travel any more without a small gold bar as a decorative necklace.

Harvey R. Wasserman

Burke, Idaho

"SHORT HAIR CUT and a beer, please." Where else but in Burke, Idaho? I was in Burke waiting for car parts to be shipped from Detroit for my broken car.

Imagine a narrow valley edged by high mountains loaded with lead and sliver ore. The rail line for the ore trains went right down the centre of Main Street, and cars had to get out of the way. A short tunnel was cut through the hotel that fed and housed the miners. Food was excellent, straightforward and plentiful (steak, bacon and eggs, piled high), free for the miners. One morning, at restaurant prices I ate $60 worth of bacon. The hotel rooms were clean, spartan and comfortable.

Up before dawn with a lamp on our hard helmets, we sat on open flatbed rolling stock. Planks of wood were our seats. We were pulled through a long, low tunnel into the heart of the mountain by an electrified engine. Nothing was insulated, and the sparks flying from the bare wire that powered us created an intermittent scary lighting. We ended up in a huge cavern where elevators awaited us.

This was the Hercules Mine. It was being excavated upwards. The elevator was on two levels, each crammed with six miners packed in like sardines. There was no protection in the front of the elevator. Tilting twenty degrees backward, the elevator climbed rapidly and let miners off at the "drift" (shaft) where they were working.

I was assigned to work with Bob at the nine hundred foot level. Bob was experienced and worked the mines one year to pay for his next year at college. Our drift was mined out but contained wooden shafts from upper levels stuffed with ore.

Our job was to fill individual V-shaped carts with the ore. We pushed them to the end of the drift and dumped them down a huge cavity, two hundred feet wide, down to ground level.

Sometimes rock jammed in the shafts. Dynamite tied to a stick, lit and thrown up the shafts, run like hell, took care of the problem. I had no waterproof footwear. One-and-a-half inches of water between the ore car rails. I had to tightrope walk on the rails to keep my feet dry.

I had a long steel rod, no dynamite, for the shaft at the end of the ore cart run. Two rocks got stuck. I pried them and they moved, holding the rod and lifting me toward the ore hole. I tried to free the rod until I realised it was me or the rod. I just let go at the edge, letting the rod fall nine hundred feet.

There was a fifteen-minute elevator ride to lunch at the eleven hundred foot level. Lunch was allowed for thirty minutes, and then it was another fifteen minute ride back to our drift.

To keep the unions out, they paid us $28 a day, good wages at the time. Along with the regular pay was portal-to-portal pay, meaning that we worked an eight-hour day, three-and-a-half hours of which were spent getting to and from our worksite.

Saturday and Sunday were free. On the side of the only street were seven shops, four bars, one liquor store, a barbershop with a bar in the back and a clothing store with the inevitable bar.

Saturday night the miners got drunk, fought and recovered on Sunday.

I was 19, so I only called and told my mother when I left. Over the phone came "Oy! Gevalt! Kensuch Gehargen Veren!" shouted by my ten-year-old Yiddish-speaking cousin. "Oh my God, you could get killed!"

Attacked In Africa

I VOLUNTEERED to give a lecture at a World Health Organisation hospital in central Nigeria.

I had feelings of anxiety about lecturing to a large international audience. I was afraid if my presentation was attacked I wouldn't be able to handle such an assault gracefully. The participants in this meeting were black Nigerian psychiatrists trained in Scotland and a large group of psychiatrists from all over the world, especially Europe.

I decided to give the most controversial speech I could so that I would be attacked and could practice handling such an assault. I spoke of a psychotherapy founded on chakras, auras and energy fields. By God, I did get attacked. To my surprise, I got support from all the Europeans. I was aggressively battered by the chief of all Nigerian psychiatrists.

All I remember of his attack was, "I don't know who or what you are, Dr. Wasserman."

I handled his attack beautifully. "Sometimes I also wonder who or what I am."

I was relieved at my calm charm.

Some time later, lecturing in Arizona to an international meeting, I was so anxious that I forgot my most important point. I managed to recover and save myself. I was not frightened in central Nigeria. I was frightened in central United States.

After the meeting in Nigeria the hospital gave us a cocktail party. I wanted to socialise with the head of psychiatry. Even though he attacked me, he was a lovely man. Every time I approached him, he walked across the room away from me.

I subsequently found out he was not only head psychiatrist of Nigeria but also a hereditary tribal chieftain. At times he had to perform ancient ceremonies, including cutting a sheep's throat while uttering magical phrases and using the blood for healing. I guess my speech was a threat to his desire to be a modern and scientific psychiatrist.

I was rescued at the end of the meeting by a black psychiatrist, the head of the hospital. After the party he drove me to my hotel. His father was a Yoruba tribesman. His mother was a black Falashan Jew from Ethiopia. In Judaism, you inherit your religion through your mother, so he considered himself Jewish. When he found out I was Jewish, he became very friendly and gave me the history of Jews in Ethiopia.

King Solomon visited the Queen of Sheba in Ethiopia and fathered a child with her, Menelik the First. He became the first Jewish king of Ethiopia. This sophisticated, black, Jewish royal dynasty persisted until about the year 1600. They were overthrown and became poor craftsmen.

In recent times, the left-wing government of Ethiopia persecuted the Jews, and the Israeli government secretly flew most of them to Israel. When they heard the plane loudspeakers, they thought it was the voice of God. On one plane they wanted to start a cooking fire on the floor of the plane.

At first, the Ethiopian Jews were not accepted by the conservative Jews in Israel. They didn't speak Hebrew. They spoke Aramaic, which was the language of Jesus and all ancient Jews. They knew only the ancient texts of the Bible, not the more recent holy Jewish books.

I sent money to finance the rescue and have followed the fate of the Ethiopian Jews in Israel. They now are fully accepted, are fantastic artists and take to the computer like Western children. They need a lot of health care and exposure to Western education.

Trip To Igasu Falls

IGASU FALLS is in a remote area of Brazil and is one of the most magnificent waterfalls in the world. Higher than Niagara, the falls make a gentle horseshoe shape and are surrounded by jungle. Until they built an airport near the falls, it was difficult to reach.

I flew to Assuncion, Paraguay, and rented a car. It was an old American Dodge with a push button shift that fell into the dashboard the first time I pushed it into high gear. I drove across Paraguay with only one gear, fourth gear. Paraguay was run by a ruthless dictator named Strasser. There were military checkpoints every twenty miles.

At the border with Brazil was a hotel. I crossed the border only to find that the dirt road to the falls was being reconstructed. The reconstructed road was about ten feet wide with a ditch three feet deep on either side of the road.

As I drove, it started to get dark. The road was scary. Natives with machetes appeared whenever I stopped to look around.

I decided to return to the hotel at the Paraguayan border. I had no reverse gear.

I turned the wheel counterclockwise after placing the nose as far clockwise as I could. My children and wife pushed the car backward. I helped by sitting in the car with one foot on the ground, pushing through the open door.

We could only do this manoeuvre safely for about a foot and a half or two feet. Then I slammed on the brake and turned the wheel clockwise, and we carried out the same procedure pushing the car forward. It was frightening to move the car as far as we could without going into that ditch. It took fifteen such manoeuvres to turn the car around one hundred and eighty degrees.

Back to the hotel. The hotel was nice, with good food and a casino that allowed children to gamble on the slot machines.

I decided to teach my two sons the foolishness of gambling. I gave them each a handful of coins, certain that they would lose them all. One son scored a big hit, and the second a jackpot. They playfully sneered at me, "So you only lose at gambling, Dad. Ha!"

Next day at breakfast we met an American couple with a jeep. They were also going to Igasu Falls. He was a water engineer. He not only offered to drive us to the falls but informed me never to drink bottled water in a third world country, only carbonated water that requires technology. The bottle can easily be rinsed and filled with polluted water (beer also is a safe bet).

Our trip with our new companions was uneventful except for a clearing in the jungle of about one acre, filled with intensely beautiful blue and purple iridescent butterflies.

At the falls there was a decent hotel and a possible trip by rowboat to a rock that hung over the falls.

The rowboat on this precarious-looking trip was served by an elderly local with muscles of steel. He made it to the rock and chained the boat to the rock. The vibrating rock was fifteen feet long and three or four feet wide, overhanging the falls by three or four feet.

The view was overwhelmingly magnificent. I enjoyed it until my children ran to the tip of the rock over the falls. I grabbed them and forced them to sit, straddling the rock at its point that was poised dramatically over the falls. I denied myself a similar pleasure but examined cracks in the rock and discovered many semi-precious stones.

The Igasu River flows through an area of Brazil called Minas Gerias (General Mines) full of semi-precious stones.

Our new friends drove us back to the border hotel and left.

Our car was parked on top of a small hill. The damn battery was dead. "La Batteria No Hay Fuerza" brought no help from anyone. There was only one chance. If I could roll our car down the hill, when it picked up speed the clutch might engage and start the engine. This usually doesn't work on a car that has an automatic transmission. There was a miracle. It worked.

I could only do this once. I had to drive across Paraguay and never stop or stall the engine.

A log-carrying cart crossed the road. I barely missed it. Stopping at a midway gas station was a careful manoeuvre. At this one gas station, I filled the tank with the engine running. I bought bottles of orange soda for everybody to drink to fight off the jungle heat. Every bottle was filled with flies.

I made it through the military checkpoints without stalling the engine.

When we returned our car to the rental agency, they wanted more money. We were four hours later than we had contracted for. I refused, screaming. Aided by a dictionary, I shouted in Spanish, "The car is a moving hearse."

I fled by taxi to the airport, afraid that the dictator's relatives would be the ones running the car rental agency and I'd end up behind bars.

Finally our plane took off.

The Fatal Lie

DON WAS A FAMOUS PSYCHOPATH at the West Haven VA Hospital. He was so talented as a psychopath that he was kept on the acute psychotic locked ward. He could lie and manipulate with incredible skill. He had committed many crimes, including rape. He even managed to get a female patient on a locked ward pregnant. He was able to get mute, isolated, psychotic patients to sign petitions, even patients who refused to talk to the staff doctors.

The treatment plan for Don was to catch all his manipulations and take away privileges one by one. Examples of privileges included swimming, dances, petty money allowance. We were hoping he would want his privileges back, encouraging good behaviour. It was a waste of time. As I was a new psychiatric trainee, I was placed in charge of the acute psychotic ward that included Don.

The previous trainee had managed to delay confronting Don for several pieces of bad behaviour. The bastard left it to little old me, little old untrained me, to handle it. I screwed up my courage and confronted him several times, removing privilege after privilege in the face of his brilliant aggressive attempts to make me feel guilty and uncomfortable with what I was doing. One of the conditions was that he was forbidden to meet or communicate with the lady he got pregnant.

The hospital design was a series of corridors. Each ward was entered from the corridor by a locked door. On entry, you found yourself in the area where staff offices and facilities were located. This ended in another locked door that opened to the patients' living quarters, an open ward.

One fine day, the patients were all at some activity. The rest of the staff was also off the ward. I stayed in my office to do paper work. Taking a short break, I strolled in the staff corridor. I saw a note slowly slip under the door from the main corridor.

I picked it up. Oh my God! It was a note from the girl-friend naming a place and time for the next meeting.

I could not face confronting him once again. My fragile beginner's personality was too weak. No one knew I had remained in my office. I tore up the note.

A day later Don asked for a private consultation in my office. "Did you pick up a note that came in for me yesterday?"

"No, I didn't," I lied.

He questioned again. I lied again. He didn't call me a liar, but I could sense that I had hurt this accomplished psycho-pathic liar by lying to him. I had hurt a patient in a lie, even though he was a committed, conscious-less, professional liar!

Thank you, Don. He taught me that lying to a patient is unforgivable. Of course!

It destroys a treatment that relies on one premier essential, TRUST.

I never lied to a patient again. You can make some mistakes in a patient-doctor relationship and be forgiven, but never a lie.

CHAPTER ELEVEN

THE HUMAN HEART

Our Anger Destroys Our Loved Ones

LET ME PRESENT a radical and difficult idea. Anger, especially rage, has no place in an intimate relationship, no place with children, no place between partners, lovers, husbands and wives.

The intimate relationship between a man and a woman is a setting where rage and anger are totally harmful and inappropriate. What is necessary is the sharing of emotions, as part of clear and honest communication. Since anger is mainly based on fear and emotional pain, partners should be expressing fear and emotional pain.

If there is love, the partner will respond compassionately. We care about those we love if they are frightened, we care about those we love when they are in pain. If this does not happen, the relationship is extremely troubled. A partner who cannot respond creates a doomed relationship.

Compassion for your partner's fear and pain is dramatically healing.

If you have been in a relationship contaminated by deep anger, problems rarely get solved: negative reactions can last for hours, days, months, even indefinitely. In situations where the communication about a problem is clear, simple, honest and compassionate, problems are solved quickly. They are listened to because compassion is the music of love.

Content can be heard, but shared compassionate emotion must take precedence over content. Then content can be responded to constructively. You are no longer afraid to speak up. The time of living in the misery of endless, futile, battling anger is diminished, even ended.

There is only one truly legitimate reason for anger; such anger is called *entitlement anger*. Let me explain. Anger is devised by nature to raise our ability to enter into combat, or perhaps to flee in the face of an attack on vital aspects of our life. Anger is designed to be there if somebody tries to harm you or your children. Anger is there to help you if someone wants to destroy your means of livelihood. When an angry mother grizzly bear rises on her hind legs to her full 10-12 muscular feet, it is because she is there to protect her baby from a perceived danger. All this is entitlement anger.

Most of what we call anger is really covering fear and pain. People feel energised and powerful in anger; gone is the vulnerability of fear and emotional pain. Intimate murderers are deeply hurt; they kill in the anger that buries their emotional pain.

If a stranger is angry, that's just unpleasant. But with a lover, a close friend, a parent, we are open and vulnerable at a very deep level. Anger that penetrates to that level sears our very essence, sears and burns our soul and leaves scars that may never heal.

Rage in relationships is usually, but not exclusively, a male expression. A raging father has devastating effects. Children become afraid of their father. It can produce in girls an antipathy to the entire male gender. Great anger plus intimacy is devastating. The devastated partner loses self-esteem and becomes afraid of doing anything that will bring forth the rage. Love and respect wither. Marital fights are usually power struggles, and raging power struggles resolve nothing. Intimacy anger is incredibly powerful and destructive to those who care about you, to those whom you say you love.

In a lot of families that I work with, the father's anger has been the dominant factor in family life. The wife often is depressed and intimidated. The children's self-esteem is low. They escape from the family as soon as they are old enough.

John and his wife and five children came to see me. I was amazed at the ferocity and intensity of John's rage. He was totally unaware of the intensity of his rage and the devastating effect it had on his family. However, basically he was a caring person, and so he quickly copped on and got his anger under control. He listened more and understood what was happening in his family. He became a sensitive and emotionally reactive father. Great healing took place in the family.

After family therapy, I have seen several of the children who were still deeply scarred by their father's earlier "rage parenting."

With a parent who won't change, if they are addicted to their anger, the family will continue to deteriorate or disintegrate.

When the offending parent, the raging, outrageous parent, is aware and shocked at the intense effect their anger has and wants to do something about it, almost immediately that awareness begins to diminish their anger. For a while they are confused and do not know the best way to interact and respond to those close to them. With time and a bit of therapeutic help, they find other ways of dealing with family problems and are delighted with a happier, communicating and co-operating family.

If you know someone who has problems with intense anger in any situation, or if you have problems yourself, here is a simple exercise that may help.

When you are alone, allow yourself to bring up or remember a situation that produced intense anger. Let yourself go into it as strongly and powerfully as you can and then look at yourself in a mirror. You may be shocked. Make a tape recording of your anger and sense what it feels like to receive such toxic emotion.

The following exercise may also be helpful. Every day when you are alone, let loose your anger for 30 or 45 seconds. Feel the full intensity of it. Then drop the anger and let your mind go to some beautiful, peaceful, wonderful experience — a beautiful sunset or a field of flowers. Always stay in the positive mental state for at least five or ten times longer than the anger.

Your anger is deeply encoded in the pathways of your mind. You are attempting to restructure those pathways.

Repeat this over and over again for about five or ten minutes each day.

Current research with brain imaging shows that even as we get older there is a phenomenon that is called neuroplasticity.

This simply means that the pathways in your mind can be changed. Dramatic awareness makes it possible for those pathways to change.

In a small percentage of people, anger can be secondary to physical, medical and neurological problems, so a work-up from your General Practitioner may also be useful.

The Heart Roots Exercise

LIVE WITH A WOUNDED HEART, and you will live your life crippled. The heart roots exercise can be an important step in your healing. I dedicate this exercise to my grandma, Miriam. In the four years she was in my life, she taught me about love, unconditional love.

This nursing exercise is based on Chinese medicine. The value to children of nursing is not only for food, but for the warm, soothing feeling it produces at the base of their hearts.

Start this exercise by nursing vigorously on the soft fleshy tissue at the base of your thumb. Nurse vigorously like a hungry baby until you feel the warmth. If this does not happen, or if you feel uncomfortable nursing, imagine warmth at the base of your heart. Reinforce the flow of the warmth from the base of the heart throughout this exercise.

Nourished by the warmth at the base of your heart, visualise a root growing slowly from your heart down your chest, through your abdomen, into your pelvis, where the root divides in two, growing down through your thighs, your knees, your legs, your ankles, your feet and deep into the ground beneath you.

Take a few moments to energise your heart roots with your warmth. Now allow the warmth to produce an elaborate, deep, multi-branched root system, deep in the ground beneath your feet. Take a few minutes to nourish the root system you have developed.

Now produce small but complete root systems in each part of your body that the main root has passed through; your chest, pelvis, thighs, knees, legs, ankles, feet. Do this slowly and gently, and allow the nourishing warmth from the base of your heart to cause smaller but rich root systems to develop in every part of your body that the root has passed through.

When this rich root system nourished by heart warmth is completed, take a few minutes to remain conscious of the complete root system being nourished by the heart warmth.

Harvey R. Wasserman

Stop all deliberate conscious activity. How do you feel? You probably feel calmer, stronger, less vulnerable. Get up and walk around. Does your body feel stronger, more vigorous? Do you feel more engaged with the ground beneath your feet?

Repeat this exercise once or twice daily for six weeks so that the healing effect can become a part of your personality, your life, your very heart.

The Heart Chant

MUSIC can be strengthening and healing. Chant the three sounds I suggest for ninety seconds each, slowly raising and lowering the pitch several times.

1. OHM. The central pitch of this sound should be felt in the front of the chest centred at a central point one-third of the way up from the bottom of your sternum.

2. YAM. The tone should be adjusted to locate itself in the centre of the chest just behind the location for the sound of OHM.

3. AWE. A deeper sound made at the back of the throat, mouth wide open in an oval shape with the sides of the mouth brought in to about half or three-quarters of an inch wide. The sound should be located at the same latitude as the other two but in your back, centred on your spine.

Repeat this series at least three times, and see how you feel. You probably will notice that your chest feels warmer and your heart feels more open and radiant.

Harvey R. Wasserman

Heart Chakra Stimulation*

IN THE CENTRE of your sternum and up about one-third from the bottom of your sternum is a small tender spot. This is the heart chakra.

Place the centre of the palm of your dominant hand over this area. Imagine for about forty-five seconds that you can see the area of skin under the palm of your hand.

Next, shift the imagery to a place of incredible beauty. You can imagine a sunset, a field of beautiful flowers or anything that strongly stimulates your memory of beauty. Hold this image for about forty-five seconds.

Now stop all conscious activity and see how you feel. You will probably feel yourself in a better state emotionally, and physically warmer. This lovely feeling may last ten or fifteen minutes before it fades. If repeated frequently over a period of months, some permanent effect can be achieved.

It can be helpful to use this technique for short-term results. For example, try this if you feel shut down emotionally, especially before you greet your family after a difficult day of hard work.

* [Developed by Doc Childre, Institute of HeartMath]

Contacting The Nature Spirits

TWELVE psychiatrists and a guide landed at the Ivory Coast (West Africa), boarded our bus and drove for seven hours into the heart of the country, much of it through dense jungle.

We were on our way to visit a witch doctor training school. These were female white witches who communed with the nature spirits to heal illness and crop problems. In this remote African area, women had power only if they were ordained white witches. Tuition was $3,000. The course took three years.

They knew we were coming. We entered the village square, which was surrounded by thatched huts. The villagers were assembled on one side. On two sides were four large conga drums and drummers. On the fourth side were tribal carvings so beautiful a collector would die for any one of them. We were seated in front of several huts.

The conga drums began with a power and rhythm that penetrated and captured consciousness.

Then, dancing into the square between the carved figures (six feet tall), entered the professor. About forty-five years of age, she wore only a wrap-around skirt. Her skin was covered with grey ash. She danced to the drums for fifteen minutes.

Three teenage girls brought their dance into the square. Dressed like their teacher, skin covered with grey ash, each wore a bandelero of leather dangling from their shoulders covered with strange undecipherable fetishes.

The students danced with their teacher for ten minutes. Each girl then selected one of us, pinned a fetish to our clothes and invited three of us to dance. The girls chose me, my wife and one other male psychiatrist.

I am a self-conscious Western social dancer, but my spirit is liberated when dancing with tribal peoples.

Harvey R. Wasserman

There was a lot of leaping and whirling as we imitated our hostesses. I decided that like Sufi, they whirl to cancel ordinary consciousness, so nature spirits can enter them.

I jumped and whirled. I jumped and whirled in mid-air, and whenever I did a major jump whirl, the villagers shouted with excitement when I landed. I was in the flow.

After a while, I noted that the most beautiful of the girls was near me whenever my feet hit the earth.

I was entering another state of reality, coming down from my most enthusiastic leap and whirl. I landed and was facing this beautiful girl as she landed. Our eyes met. She reached and opened her wrap-around skirt, offering me a view of her genitals. She closed her skirt again and danced away.

I couldn't dance. I lost my contact with the nature spirits and shuffled over to my wife.

"Did you see what I saw?"

"Yes."

"What does it mean?"

"I don't know."

I asked the guide what it meant.

"It means, 'You please me.' "

The dancing went on for at least another fifteen minutes. I could barely move.

The drumming stopped. My colleagues started interacting with the ladies – photos, compliments, glowing in admiration.

One of the psychiatrists was a black man from New York City. He glowed with excitement and desire for the beauty who had stunned me. He focused all his attention on her. She admired a ring on his hand. He gave it to her as a gift!

He wanted his picture taken with his arm around her. As this was about to happen, she saw me, pushed him away, ran to me, embraced me with one arm and demanded pictures be taken with me.

She stayed with me until it was time to board our bus. She came to my window and threw kisses just for me.

For two days I couldn't get her picture out of my mind's eye.

Perhaps I was bewitched.

The Mating Ceremony, New Guinea

WE STUMBLED into a most unusual primeval mating ceremony.

Inside of a large hut, a group of men were seated in a circle facing inward, and a similar number of women were seated in the centre of the circle forming a circle facing the men.

The name of the ceremony as translated for us into English was "Crossem Leg and Kissum Wind."

Dancing on their seats, each couple raised and intertwined one of their legs. With intense, joyous eye contact, they sang to each other.

After several minutes the circles rotated and a new pairing began.

This continued until each man and woman had experienced contact with everyone of the opposite sex in the circles.

Intuitively they decided which partnership created the greatest voltage. Paired, they ran off and mated.

Stone Age Theatre

IN THE NEXT VALLEY to the fierce Hagen People were the Chimbu Tribe. They were softer, friendlier and sensual. Our guide arranged for them to show us theatre in the village square. When we arrived, all the people of the community were gathered around, and a place was made for us.

The theatre consisted of a series of skits that portrayed episodes from the history of the tribe. One skit started with a royal parade, part of the crowning ceremony for the chief of the tribe. The chief's wicked brother and his supporters attacked the parade. War! The wicked brother was killed.

Another skit was a boundary problem in which two citizens disagreed where their land boundaries were and got into a fight with stone axes. The fighting was so realistic it was scary. It was as good as anything I have ever seen in a Hollywood movie.

Another fight took place at a make-believe stream. At this stream a warrior was polishing an axe head. His wife was pouring water from a ceramic jug to cool off the stones and provide lubrication while he was sanding the axe head into shape. A warrior nearby was doing the same thing, but nobody was helping him. After a while the wife started pouring water for the unaccompanied gentleman. Her husband took umbrage at this and started a fight with the warrior who had made his wife unfaithful. Again it was a vigorous, realistic fight with stone axes. Suddenly they stopped. After some negotiation, the husband sold his wife to her boyfriend.

Another skit portrayed a time when food was scarce. People ran around with clubs killing mice and rats, which they cooked and ate.

A pyramidal stack of reeds was in the centre of the town square. In a grand finale, the stack became a beehive attacked by sweets-starved warriors. Six bees who had been crouched in the hive for at least an hour and forty-five minutes attacked and drove away the warriors. The audience screamed with joy and laughter.

Tse-Tse Flies Versus Lizards

WHILE VISITING A MASAI village, my family was invited to examine a newly built Masai hut. The floor was freshly paved with cow dung. We politely declined. Everything about their cattle is sacred to the Masai. They are considered brothers.

I bought a necklace from a young woman. Each stone represented a cow that her family owned. Cattle were the demonstration of wealth. Part of the deal was that I drive her sister to a nearby village to meet her husband.

Our passenger entered the car covered with tse-tse flies! The flies filled the car! Tse-tse flies can carry sleeping sickness!

My boys had acquired two lizards and used them as weapons to successfully attack the flies.

As the lizards snapped up the flies with their amazing tongues, the Masai lady became hysterical: "The lizards are poisonous!"

"They aren't."

Persuasion was useless. We delivered our hysterical passenger to her husband, our car cleansed of tse-tse flies.

They'll Talk To My Mom Or Dad

IT'S TAKEN ME a long time to learn how to communicate with people of cultures very different from my professional and academic background.

For example, American Indians trust no white people, so approaching an Indian with something like, "I'm Harvey and I'm glad to meet you," will result only in a polite grunt. It's better to be silent and let them observe you for hours or even days until they decide you're not dangerous.

My mother and father knew better. My mother only graduated high school. Her father had said that females didn't need to go to college. I don't think my father even finished elementary school. He had to go to work.

While watching a Hopi Harvest Dance at the First Mesa, Arizona, I only got grunts from the Indian men around me. My mother noticed that an elderly Indian woman's eyes sparkled whenever a young girl danced by. "Your granddaughter dances beautifully." Immediately we were welcomed and given gifts and beautifully coloured corn tortillas to eat.

In Jamaica, the West Indies, near an old English fort, a black man was selling primitive carvings. I tried to talk to him about the carvings and got no reply. My father walked up and asked "How do you make a living around here?" He was instantly responded to like an old friend.

The Starving Nubian Boy

I TRAVELLED TO EGYPT weeks after the Egyptians had lost their six-day war with Israel. They were particularly nervous around strategic and military targets, so we had to travel in groups with a guide. I signed on with Lindblad Travel, a unique United States travel company that always had outstanding guides and consultants.

This trip was no different. Our guide was Shafiq Farad, retired head of all Egyptian archaeology. Shafiq was warm, creative, intelligent, knowledgeable and spoke perfect English. He was working for a little extra money to flesh out his retirement comfort. Other guides came to him for answers to archaeological questions they themselves could not answer.

Shafiq, my wife and I became friendly. After a day's touring, which included lessons in reading hieroglyphics, he would take us to a site not on the itinerary or to a restaurant that produced authentic Egyptian cuisine.

One night we went for a stroll along the Nile adjacent to the ancient ruins of the Luxor Temple. It was a brilliant, full moon night. Shafiq filled us with stories of contemporary and ancient Egypt. The Egyptians hated the Russians, who treated them contemptuously as they presented Egypt with the gift of Aswan Dam.

A dark-skinned boy, skinny and appearing about eight years old, walked up to us. He spoke to Shafiq in an unfamiliar language.

"He is Nubian and welcoming you to his country. Hold out your hand."

In the palm of my right hand, the boy poured nuts from a cone made of old newspaper. I reached into my pocket for some coins.

"No!" exclaimed Shafiq. "He is welcoming you to his country, it's a gift. He'll be hurt if you offer him money."

"How old is he?"

"Fourteen."

"Why does he look so thin and young?"

"He is starving," replied Shafiq in a matter-of-fact tone.

"What is he doing here at 11:30 at night?"

"He's trying to make a few coins to feed his family."

The boy ran away. I wanted to help. What could I do? Nothing, he was out of calling range in moments. There were tears in my eyes. I still tear whenever I think of that starving, gracious boy and his generous gift welcoming me.

When the lake behind the Aswan Dam filled up, it flooded Nubian farmland. The Egyptian Government resettled the Nubians too far from the water. The Nubians were in big trouble.

Back home in New York, in *The New York Times* was an article about the plight of the Nubians. A group had formed to collect money for pumps to bring water to the Nubian farmland.

I sent the fund some money. Not for the pump, not for the Nubian agriculture, I sent the money for that sweet, generous, welcoming starving boy.

Thank God I could do a little something for him. How wonderful and moving it is for me to know that there were still human beings in this world of that little boy's calibre.

CHAPTER TWELVE

MAMA

Mama's Boy
The Vomiting Monitor
The Sexual Retard
A Hidden Barrier To Awareness
The War Of The Jewish Mothers
My Son The Doctor Needs A Suit
Bar Mitzvah With The Devil
Devastation Or Healing, Emotional Pain
Shelob The Writer
Resurrecting Goldie (An Orchid For My Mother)
Murder By Stealth
My Sister

Mama's Boy

A TWENTY-FOUR-YEAR-OLD young man's opening challenge as he sat facing me for the first time was, "I had sex with my mother on a regular basis all during my teen years. It was wonderful. I don't want to hear any professional bullshit that it harmed me. It didn't."

His presenting complaint was that he couldn't keep a relationship with a female and didn't understand what he was doing wrong.

A twenty-five-year-old hugely attractive female was the middle child with four brothers. On a scale of one to ten, she put her self-esteem at level three. "My mother ignored me; she was jealous of the attention my father paid me. My father was the only one who paid attention to me. He told me I was beautiful and smart."

There was no joy in her as she reported her father's admiration. Then a long pause and confession. "I felt funny, uncomfortable with his compliments and attention."

"Was it sexualised?"

"Yes."

"You were sexually abused?"

"Yes I was sexually abused. I spent my time at home in my room. At school I couldn't make friends with any of the girls."

After she told me that, I was uncomfortable. Going home, I was preoccupied, down and irritable.

Then I remembered. At least once a week, my mother took me into my parents' bed. I was given small sharp scissors to trim the calluses from my mother's feet. She'd groan with pleasure. Sometimes as she bathed I walked in and was allowed to wash her back as she giggled. In many ways out of bed and bath, I was led to believe that I was more important than my father (or my sister).

Harvey R. Wasserman

My release from my bad mood came when the thought crept into my mind. *I was sexually abused by my mother.* No wonder I was shy with girls. No wonder I preferred to look for excitement in the outside world. You are limited on your inward journey if there are truths that must not be faced.

At fifteen or sixteen, I masturbated a lot and was captivated by pictures of women in their undergarments in my secret Sears and Roebuck catalogue. One day after school, my mother came in from shopping. I confronted her silently, stark naked with a huge erection. She responded as if nothing unusual was happening. After a while I got the message that nothing was going to happen. I retreated to my room. The bedroom experiences with my mother stopped. It was more than three years before I was able to be comfortable while alone with a girl.

I WAS SEXUALLY ABUSED. How else did that affect the pattern of my life?

The Vomiting Monitor

MY MOTHER'S cousin's son was in my kindergarten class. He threw up frequently during the school day. I was given the honour of accompanying him to the toilet so that he would throw up aesthetically. I was very proud to be chosen.

Something seems very wrong to me now about that response.

The Sexual Retard

EVEN BY THE STANDARDS of my teenage era, I was a sexual retard. My only knowledge of female anatomy came from the Sears Roebuck underwear catalogue.

When I was fifteen, my mother and a second cousin arranged for me and the cousin's daughter to go on a date swimming in a local lake. I was worried that if I swam with her daughter in the lake, I could get her pregnant. There was no one I felt free to talk to.

After a few days of worry, I intellectually solved the problem: her mother wouldn't want her to get pregnant, my mother wouldn't want her to get pregnant, therefore swimming in a lake with her wouldn't get her pregnant.

At about the same time, I did summer scut work in Manhattan with one of my father's colleagues. They designed, marketed and cut out the patterns that my father's company sewed into women's clothing. As I swept the floors in the pattern cutting room, I could hear the cutters talk.

They talked about whorehouses. Oh my God! I somehow knew you could get a terrible disease that way. I didn't know how it was transmitted. Maybe if I touched anything they touched, I could catch it. I memorised everything they touched and avoided it.

After I had accumulated several hundred non-touch spots, I gave up. It just got too complicated, so I forgot the whole thing.

By sixteen I was in college. Most men were in the military by then. At one point, I was the only physically intact male in my class. Everyone else had volunteered or had been drafted into combat. There were hundreds of lonely and hard-up girls. Some of them came after me. In terror, I fled for my life.

I felt awkward around girls until I was nineteen. I had spent a year and a half in the navy. Everything suddenly changed for me, for no observable reason. I dated a different girl every four or five nights and really enjoyed it.

I still managed to remain a virgin until I married at age twenty-two at the end of my second year of medical school.

A Hidden Barrier To Awareness

OTAVALO is a small town in a mountainous part of Ecuador famous for its beautiful hand-knit sweaters. I instructed my wife Sarah in the dangers and awareness of South American pickpockets. I was very experienced with travel, she was not.

There are three schools for pickpockets in South America. How is that for post-graduate training? That is useful, even in a recession! They walk behind you silently and synchronise their steps to yours, your right leg forward and theirs, your left forward and theirs. This permits them to get very close to you. I keep all valuables under my shirt, a few bills in my pocket and a decoy target bum bag on my rear with apples, oranges and film.

We were walking on a side street when I sort of noticed and ignored a short, barefoot old native lady positioning herself behind me. Suddenly I heard the zipper zip open on my bum bag. I whipped around, fists at the ready, and confronted the barefoot old lady. You don't hit barefoot old ladies in the remote mountains area, so I just yelled at her. Sarah had noticed and correctly evaluated the entire dance.

"Why didn't you warn me?" I complained.

"It was so obvious! I assumed you, the expert, were aware."

'There are no female pickpockets' is a new family motto.

My mother taught me to ignore all her destructive behaviour and to think of her as only doing everything for my own good; I extended this mis-learning to all females.

I have sensed and directly confronted a male pickpocket. I have sensed a truck driver with a club coming after me from behind. I was at a Shirley Bassey concert in London and sensed danger one hour before the concert ended; it appeared on a quiet London street. All the dangerous persons I sensed were male.

Males are possibly dangerous; females are not – this is an induced blindness that has corrupted too much of my life.

The War Of The Jewish Mothers

THE KOPPELMANS lived on the fourth floor, the Wassermans on the ground floor of the same New York City apartment house. In my immigrant Jewish culture, status was as follows:

No. 1   Doctors

No. 2   God

No. 3   Scholars

No. 4   Successful Businessmen

Mama Wasserman and Mama Koppelman would meet each month with disguised tension, politely comparing their sons' report cards. If I received an A, I got twenty five cents. Each B brought ten cents. If I outdistanced Milton Koppleman, everything was doubled.

Milton and I were in the same advanced elementary school class. The highest graded student was in the first seat of the first row. The rest were seated in their grades in linear succession. The student with the lowest marks was in the last seat of the last row.

Milton and I competed for the first and second seat, first row. My memory is that he won sixty percent of the time, and I won forty percent of the time. Seats were reallocated each marking period.

At twenty, I got into medical school. We had moved and lost contact with the Kopplemans. At a family wedding, I met a young woman who knew Milton. He had not gotten into medical school.

TRIUMPH! I had finally defeated Milton.

Two weeks of triumphant ecstasy followed. Then my triumph faded and started to seem wrong.

It has taken most of my life to eliminate my competitiveness with other men. Men are raised to compete with each other. Men should help each other. Helping other men get strong and fulfilled is now one of my life's joys.

Milton, I hope you got into medical school. If I could, I'd help you.

"My Son The Doctor" Needs A Suit

A LONG, FAT ENVELOPE arrived. After two frustrating years of applications and rejections, I was accepted into Syracuse Medical School. (The rejection envelopes were small and thin; the acceptance envelope was fat and thick.)

It took me two days to recover from positive shock and open the envelope.

We were invited to a family wedding. I need a new suit. My mother took me to the Jewish lower east side of Manhattan, where good quality merchandise was to be had at decent prices. Only goyim (Christians) paid retail.

My mother picked out a nice, conservative blue suit for me. The sleeves of the jacket and cuffs of the pants needed to be altered.

"We need the suit for a wedding next Saturday."

"Impossible. We're so busy, it will take two weeks."

My mother knew her culture. "It's for my son who just was accepted into medical school."

What a change in atmosphere. A cry went out across the store. "The doctor, the doctor!"

I had my suit altered in forty-five minutes!

Bar Mitzvah With The Devil

MY MOTHER always told me my grandfather was a devil. She told me over and over, "He is a devil. He stole my mother's jewellery. He had other women." She hinted at a lot more.

My only conscious memory of him in the four years we lived in my grandparents' house before my grandmother died was when our apples were ready to be picked from the tree in the backyard. It was to be the next day.

I asked him to wake me so I could help him pick the apples. He said he would. I woke the next morning, looked out and the tree was bare of apples. I felt heartbroken and betrayed. We moved to our own apartment after my grandmother died.

I was now 13, Bar Mitzvah time for a Jewish boy. On a drizzly day my mother took me to the Jewish lower east side of Manhattan. I was to invite my grandfather to my Bar Mitzvah, an ancient coming-of-age ceremony.

In the drizzly rain, we stood opposite an apartment house, staring at the building's entrance. We stood for about an hour. A man I didn't recognise emerged.

"That's your grandfather."

I obediently crossed the street as he unfurled a very large black umbrella.

"I am your grandson, Harvey. I am inviting you to my Bar Mitzvah."

His umbrella silently descended between us. Without a word he walked away.

The pain has never left my belly.

Devastation Or Healing — Emotional Pain

WANT TO BE MISERABLE, depressed, sick, angry, constricted, full of self-loathing? Don't deal with your emotional pain. Emotional pain feels bad, so many of us repress it, don't know what to do about it and are unaware of its consequences.

What is emotional pain? Pain is injury to the part of us that loves and needs love. How can you detect emotional pain? Speak out loud the following three sentences one after the other with a brief pause in between.

"I have a lot of emotional pain in me." Pause, observe if there is any mental, emotional or body reaction.

"I don't want to know there is a lot of emotional pain in me." Any emotional or mental or body reaction?

"Nobody or nothing can make me aware of how much emotional pain is in me." A smile or laughter is a response more reliable and more healing than any sort of mental, emotional or body reaction.

What can you do about emotional pain? You can work on your emotional pain as an assist to medication or psychotherapy, or just on your own to see if you do or don't need assistance.

Crying discharges emotional pain. Emote comes from the Latin meaning to move out. Is there any memory that would help you to cry? To have full effect, the crying should be full, deep and from the centre of your belly. Does anything help you to cry? Some of Pavarotti's arias bring out a deep discharge of my emotional pain.

Make believe you're in the theatre and you're playing a part. Make the sounds of deep crying and wailing. Make them strong and from your belly. Repeat them until you can feel some relief, some discharge. This will work about as well as genuine emotional crying.

Pain visualisation is a technique I have developed to help people discharge their pain on another level. Close your eyes. Imagine that throughout your body in every tissue, cell, space and organ is a rich, deep, royal purple substance. Imagine this for about a minute. Then contaminate that rich, deep, royal purple substance with greys and blacks and olive drabs so that it becomes a deep, murky purple. Picture that for about another minute. Now imagine the light in the room has a lovely, shimmering, pearlescent, beautiful white quality. The white essence of the light enters your body, spreading throughout your body on the in-breath, and on the out-breath takes with it a small amount of the contaminating colours, the greys, the blacks, the olive drabs. Slowly over four or five minutes the rich, deep purple is revealed in every tissue, cell, space and organ. Now imagine breathing in the beautiful white light, spreading throughout your body on the in-breath. Allow a small amount of the white to remain behind when you breathe out, so the rich deep royal purple becomes lighter and lighter over about three minutes, ending up in shades of rose and/or pink and/or lavender. Rest with your eyes closed for a number of seconds. Evaluate how you feel. Do you feel more relaxed? Do you feel lighter? Can you sense that the emotional pain has somehow been lessened? If you get a good result from this visualisation, repeat it once or twice a day for six weeks. It will often give major relief to severe emotional pain.

NOTE: *The Heart Roots Exercise* in Chapter 11 is also very helpful in reducing the effects of emotional pain.

Shelob The Writer

MY MOTHER WANTED to be a writer. She never tried except through me.

Goldie manipulated me in all possible ways to create her-son-the-doctor. She told my first wife, "Harvey was carefully engineered."

"Harvey, when you grow up, be a businessman. Make lots of money. At five o'clock you go home, all the tensions of the day are relieved, and you can enjoy your evenings, your weekends, your vacations. But it's so wonderful to be a doctor and help people. But be a businessman."

A peculiar part of her engineering me to create her son the doctor was writing all my school compositions until I went to university. "I have never been to university, so I can't continue this. You have to do it from now on." When my sixth grade teacher praised "my" writing and told me that it was so good that I should consider writing as a career, Goldie glowed with pride.

I had to write papers at university, medical school, and psychiatric residency. My professorship at Yale University College of Medicine, Department of Psychiatry, stagnated – I didn't publish. I was an outstanding teacher and administrator, but that didn't matter.

My problem was never with the content of my writing. It was with the rest of it. I had to write papers over and over before they were accepted. I devised schemes around my curse. In medical school I once wrote a paper on hirtsutism (hairiness) in women. I was certain that no one on the faculty knew anything about it. I also guessed correctly that they would be so satisfied with the information content that they would ignore the rest. (What is the one place women only grow hair if they have a testosterone-secreting tumour? THE EARS.)

My psychiatric training graduation thesis was about predicting future homicide in hospitalised patients after they were discharged. Interesting, important, original — and I hired an English teacher to re-write it. My bestselling book, *The Healing Road*, was based on five outstanding lectures. I am one hell of an outstanding lecturer. Thousands of people jammed into auditoriums to hear my lectures that ended up as that book.

When I began to write a sequel, I became anxious, with an illogical intrusive thought that I would die if I finished my second book. The next morning, I woke up. When I looked in the mirror, one-half of my face was paralysed. I had Bell's palsy, caused by pressure on the facial nerve as it leaves the skull. I have no doubt in my mind that the terror I experienced the night before and the paralysis of my face were directly related to my attempt at writing.

I am determined to destroy this limiting, negative and destructive script in my unconscious mind. I have forced myself to write, with lots of encouragement from my present wife. The result was beautiful writing plus horrendous nightmares and frequent anxiety attacks. Every time I was forced to stop writing, I had to force myself through my procrastination to start writing again. The writing itself has miraculously become easy and enjoyable. When my friend, author and teacher of writing, David Rice, told me I had a potential bestseller, my celebration was a panic attack.

You will never overcome the prohibitions in your life, often implanted before memory, without the experience of anxiety and the determination to continue through the centre of your anxious suffering. Follow me, my friends, follow me through the centre of your prohibitions and limitations. Follow me through the anxiety to freedom and fulfilment.

Resurrecting Goldie (An Orchid for My Mother)

PSYCHODRAMA is a form of psychotherapy in which people in your life and parts of your personality are played by others. Integration, awareness, healing and resolution are stimulated by the director (therapist).

When I was about eight, I won a scholarship to study the violin. Sometimes my mother accompanied me on the piano located in the guest living room. I missed the same note three times. Goldie produced a men's wooden suit hanger and broke the dowel part over my back. I tried harder. Everything my mother did was for my good.

Forty years later, I was a protagonist (patient) at a psychodrama about this event. At the point where I was assaulted, instead of a coat hanger the psychodramatist used a sleeve of Styrofoam cups, not a coat hanger. I swung around fast, clenched my fist ready to kill my assailant. I thank God the Styrofoam caused no pain, or in a single rage-propelled blow I would have killed "Goldie." I had never known such rage.

The next day my psychotherapist asked me, "Do you think your mother was cruel?"

"No."

Something then shifted in my head. If anyone treated my sons as I had been treated, it certainly would be cruel. MY MOTHER WAS CRUEL!

She broke a coat hanger over my back when I tore my pants playing. MY MOTHER WAS CRUEL.

Once I made a small stain on the wall with an over-ripe banana. Goldie grabbed a huge knife, pulled down her blouse and bra, and indented the knife in her breast for over an hour. My sister and I pleaded with her not to kill herself. MY MOTHER WAS CRUEL.

I was raised to be a patriotic citizen. As I reached military age, Goldie found a man who would remove one of my testicles. I couldn't say no. I managed to indicate no. Then there was a man who would give me pills to create an undiagnosed fever. I couldn't say no. I indicated no. Goldie showed no awareness of how such proposals would traumatise a teenage boy. MY MOTHER WAS CRUEL.

In his long-hair hippy phase, my youngest son hitchhiked 2500 miles to visit his sick grandma, Goldie, in Florida. She wouldn't let him in her apartment. Conform or you're out. MY MOTHER WAS CRUEL.

Goldie bragged that I had been toilet trained by the time I was 11 months old. No child of that age can be toilet trained without cruelty. MY MOTHER WAS CRUEL.

In a therapy group I ran, I asked patients to imagine they were suffering every cruelty inflicted on infants. When it came to imagine shaking an infant to death I, the therapist, was the only one to respond with a panicked reaction. Had something happened? Was Goldie that cruel?

In my life I found myself accepting abuse from women much more than from men. Is that why I had to work so hard on anxiety? Is that why when I try to break out of Goldie's mould for my future, I find it so difficult?

Today I thought, *Goldie, I want to kill you. I hate you.* My entire body shook in panic.

Is this my healing, my retrieving all of my soul?

When I achieve this, I can forgive you and feel my love for you.

Murder By Stealth

MY MOTHER killed my father and he allowed it.

I met them in El Paso, Texas, on a tour of the US southwest. My father was very senile. At dinner I noticed that my mother took the menu away from him and told him what he would eat.

I began to sit between them and let my dad choose his own food. He immediately seemed less senile.

At the El Paso airport, where we were to take the next flight on our tour, we were bumped due to overbooking of the flight. My "senile father" disappeared and returned ten minutes later. He had convinced the flight manager to bump another family. We were on our way to Las Vegas.

We checked into the fourteenth floor of the Dunes Hotel. My father was becoming less and less senile.

One afternoon he started to tell Goldie all the things in their marriage he didn't like. She became angry and hysterical, threw one leg over the balcony and threatened to jump if he didn't stop.

He stopped and became more confused.

She cancelled the rest of the trip and booked a flight back to their home in Miami.

My father hated the work he had to do to support us during the years of the Depression.

A few years before this notorious trip to the southwest, he became a partner in a beautiful residence hotel on an island in Biscayne Bay, Miami. His job was to rent the properties and deal with any tenant problems. People immediately liked and respected my dad.

During a deep recession, they alone of all such properties were completely booked. People intuitively trusted my dad, and rented. He spent part of each day socialising with the tenants,

Harvey R. Wasserman

talking, drinking tea, playing cards. If there was a problem, he fixed it. They renewed their rental. For the first time in his life Dad enjoyed his work and was making good money.

My mother complained. "How can I respect a man that plays all day?"

She forced him to sell sometime before our southwest tour. His senility began.

After leaving Las Vegas, my father's senility increased. It was not long before he was in a nursing home. Soon after that, he died.

Just before he died I had my first, last and only deep, loving hug with my father.

My Sister

"I NEVER quote my mother – she had a lot of crazy ideas."

Not being the favourite child has its advantages.

CHAPTER THIRTEEN

SEARCHING FOR A FATHER

Searching For A Father

I KNEW I WAS LOOKING for some successful man to take me under his wing so I would grow strong and powerful. The little promising chick nurtured by the big powerful rooster.

I was good at getting strong, powerful, successful men interested in me. They did give me important learning and teaching experiences. There always was a price. The last one was Dr. Al Lowen, the developer of bioenergetic analysis therapy, a therapy that combines psychoanalysis with body work. I was being groomed to be important in his organisation. Plum assignments and key workshops were mine. One day, in a moment of unexpected honesty, I told Al in a therapy session with me that I wouldn't be an exclusive bioenergetic therapist. I would use all he had taught me but would broaden my work.

On leaving Al's therapy room, he gave patients a card for the next appointment. Arriving at my office, I noticed he hadn't given me one. I called to remind him. He gave me an appointment. In his voice, I heard that he didn't want to. I thought about it for one or two days and cancelled.

A little adult fathering can be useful, but it only works its miracles during your growth years. If you keep looking, you stay little. It's time to step out into the world and become your own good father.

Getting To Know My Father

I BARELY REMEMBER my father until I was almost a teenager. There is a picture of me aged five on his lap. I always view it like it was taken on Mars.

At seven, I had to spend a night in a bed with him at a resort when the reservations got mixed up. I stayed awake all night in terror that he would touch me. I propped myself at the very edge of the bed, one hand on the ground so I wouldn't fall.

At about eight or nine, I heard him cry on his way to a cancer centre. The lump in his throat proved benign.

In New York City you cannot work until you are sixteen. I was twelve, over six feet and wanted to have some money. This was the Great Depression. My father could pay me out of petty cash, thus avoiding legal problems.

He said "No!"

"Why?"

"I have worked all my life, and you don't have to work yet. I don't want you to work until you have to."

I got my mother on my side. He surrendered. (There is a definition of a family as a dictatorship run by the sickest person.)

He overworked and underpaid me. I knew he wanted me to quit. I wasn't going to.

In midsummer he relented, doubled my pay and bought me treats for lunch. I got to know my father as I had never known him before. He, not his partner, made his little clothing factory work. He negotiated price with the machine operators of every race. They listened and liked my father.

I collected workers' salaries in a lunch bag from the bank on Fridays. (Gangsters wouldn't expect a kid to carry all that money in a brown paper bag.) As I walked through the garment district, people in his trade called me by his name, "Charlie," as they walked behind me. I was his height, shape and colouring. I could tell as they called out, "Charlie," that he was liked and respected.

Swearing me to secrecy, he played a complicated card game called pinochle on Saturdays. I was not to tell my mother. He was master at the game and made fifteen to twenty-five dollars every Saturday, important money during the Depression.

My father was worthy of the respect and admiration my mother had never taught me.

My Professor

HE WAS BRILLIANT, creative, kind, loving, outstanding at his work and a great teacher. He was Professor Alfred Francis Huettner, my professor of embryology at Queens College in the City of New York.

The year I graduated from college was the most difficult year for getting accepted to medical school, because that year all the people who had suspended their applications due to World War II applied at once.

All my applications were rejected. Professor Huettner took charge. "Stay in college for one more year. I will get you into medical school. Only apply to the schools I tell you to."

These were medical schools where he had taught or where there were professors he had done research with at the Woods Hole Oceanographic Institute.

"Only get letters of recommendation from the professors I suggest."

These were faculty members where he could read and control the content of the letters.

"Wear a clean, pressed blue suit, white shirt, conservative blue tie, polished leather shoes. Sit up. Don't slouch or cross your legs. They will ask you many questions, but the important one is, why do you want to be a doctor."

Can you guess the correct answer? If your answer was wanting to help people, you're wrong. Medical schools had painfully discovered that idealistic students didn't have the stamina to complete four years of intensely difficult, grinding years of study.

The correct answers are: (1) I am very interested in science; (2) I will be able to apply science in my practice; (3) I will make a decent living; (4) it's a plus to be able to be helping people at the same time.

When I gave my well-rehearsed correct answer, the committee members all relaxed and smiled.

Ten days later, a large, fat envelope arrived. I knew I had been accepted. The dozen rejection letters were all in small thin envelopes. I looked at it but wouldn't open that big fat envelope for two days. I had to wait for the shock to wear off. It was replaced with joy.

My father sent Professor Huettner six blouses that he manufactured, to thank him. I wanted to repay his kindness and belief in me with high grades. I was the first student he had recommended that was accepted to my medical school. If I did well, they would honour his recommendations. I was successful.

Doctor Love And My Life

IN THE MIDDLE-CLASS Jewish culture I was raised in, the highest social standing was accorded to physicians. Just below that was God, followed by scholars and then successful businessmen.

Glory struck. I was accepted to Syracuse University College of Medicine.

I instantly knew I was going to be THE WORLD'S GREATEST DIAGNOSTIC PHYSICIAN. I would find out what was wrong with people when no one else could.

Syracuse was not a happy medical school. The faculty were not very friendly. One professor would greet you in the hall sneering, "Good morning, Doctor." Translated, his remark was, "So you think you are going to be a doctor?" You immediately shrank three sizes. What was worse was if he ignored you and said nothing. We had many exams but were never given grades. If you were doing badly, the long arm of the Dean would grab you by the throat and drag you to his office.

Five students were asked to give lectures at the beginning of the second year of medical school. I was one of them. I knew I must have done reasonably well. They asked me to lecture on a very complicated topic that we had never covered in class, the inflammatory process. Consistent with the school's policy of keeping you as tense as possible, I was given my topic at 3 pm, and the lecture was to be delivered the next morning at 9 am. I stayed up all night reading and studying. My lecture went over well with students and faculty.

Third year medical school was focused on clinical diagnostic medicine. I studied incessantly and worked harder on the wards than I needed to. I accumulated and mastered textbooks five to ten years ahead of my third year medical status.

Mount Sinai Medical School was the world centre of diagnostic medicine. They chose nine students to work there during summer vacation. If they liked you, they would accept you for an internship. You would be tutored by an outstanding faculty. I was one of the nine students chosen from throughout the United States. My dream was taking shape. My dream was happening.

In the week before I had to start at Mount Sinai, I received a postcard from the Dean of Syracuse Medical School that I was "conditioned in medicine," or in other words, I DID NOT PASS THE COURSE!

I rushed up to Syracuse and met with the Dean. He knew me not. He had only been a professor speaking to us from the lecture platform.

"Why was I conditioned?"

"You were disrespectful to your superiors."

"I was never disrespectful to my superiors. I was where I most wanted to be. I thought I was home."

He did not like my answer defending my truth. He was going to support his staff member. He knew me not.

At my medical school, they kicked you out for attitude and behaviour. As an example, one male medical student was discharged because he was "living in sin" with a female. I knew my career was vibrating on a knife edge.

I spontaneously reinvented the Chinese confession (a convincing lie to please the possible executioner). After a dramatic, prolonged, thoughtful pause, I confessed. "You know, you are right. How fortunate that this defect in my character was identified this early in my career so that it can be corrected."

I was lying through my teeth.

The broad smile on the professor's face told me that my lie was accepted, and my stay in medical school was safe.

I had to resign from Mount Sinai. I was assigned to a summer class with students who were academic flunkies. We were to be supervised over the summer by DOCTOR LOVE. I had been in small group seminar with Doctor Love. I knew it had been Dr. Love who conditioned me in medicine.

Before medical school, I went to a wonderful, free New York City college, Queens College. We were encouraged to question and disagree with professors. The best teacher I ever had would ask a question containing deliberate false information to make certain that you had studied and understood. He would playfully embarrass you if you agreed with him. This course was in the field of genetics. In my medical school I was much better prepared in genetics than anyone from any of the Ivy League schools because I was taught to study, to think and to listen constructively.

In the fall I asked my friends who had been in the seminar with Doctor Love if they saw me being disrespectful. "No" was the universal answer. "He didn't like you correcting him, showing that you knew more biochemistry than he did." (Thank you, Queens College!)

I asked my friends why they didn't tell me. "It was so obvious that you must have seen it; if you decided that you wanted to go ahead, it was your right to do that."

I was wrong. I was not in my spiritual and emotional home. It is fine to dream, but always with one eye on reality or you may be destroyed.

I spent the worst summer of life, kissing everybody's ass and doing more dirty work than I was supposed to.

At one point Doctor Love made a biochemical error, and I started to correct him. At mid-sentence I turned the sentence around so that I agreed with him. I didn't give a damn if all those other students had defective biochemical information; it was survival time.

I was upset and looked for a new dream.

After a prolonged search, I found the Menninger Foundation School of Psychiatry, the best in the world. At Menninger's, I had the most happy personal and educational experience of my life.

In retrospect, I believe psychiatry suits my personality better than internal medicine. It is an honour to be in a field where human beings trust me with their tortured lives, their very tortured souls, hoping for help. I relish being in a discipline where the main questions are: What is the true nature of mankind? How do we get ourselves into so much trouble and suffering? How can you help somebody get out?

I was trained to be a soldier and carry on, and so I did. Sixty years later, after a brilliant performance of Verdi's "Don Carlos," my pain surfaced. I cried in despair for three hours.

No More Teachers

AMERICAN DOCTORS weren't helping me with a chronic medical problem. In the local papers I spotted an announcement that England's most admired and respected spiritual healer would be available locally in one week.

I called the listed phone number and found that he would not only be in my office building but in the very office next to mine. My landlord occupied the next office. (To my surprise, he was not only interested in money but also in spiritual healing.)

The gods had spoken. I made an appointment. My English healer proved to be a very pleasant gentleman. He made no impact on my medical problem. But from out of nowhere (he knew nothing about me) he said, "You don't need any more teachers."

This hit me like a thunderbolt. I knew he was absolutely right. I immediately broke contact with my virtual father figure teachers and all my other teachers.

The result was a dramatic and precious increase in my creativity.

CHAPTER FOURTEEN

DOCTORING

The Glamour Of Being A Doctor

EACH OF HER BREASTS was as large as and shaped like a big bag of flour. They hung to her waist.

It was my second year in medical school. This was my first patient physical examination. All went well until it was time to do a cardiac examination. Her heart was well hidden under her breasts. *How do I get there?*

I screwed up my courage and slid my hand and stethoscope under her breast. It was wet, sweaty, slippery and revolting. I was nauseated. I barely stopped myself from vomiting.

I am supposed to be a doctor. I hung in there until I heard every last heart sound.

On extracting my polluted hand, I searched for my superior and told him what had happened.

"Not a problem."

He went up to her and casually flipped her breasts over her shoulder.

There is so much to learn in medicine.

Harvey R. Wasserman

The Hell Of Neurosurgery

THANK GOD, only two weeks on neurosurgery. I was a hardworking, dedicated intern until my first scrub on a brain operation.

All I was to do was hold two retractors to keep the scalp from falling in and covering the field of the operation. There were four besides me at the operating table, so I had to stand sideways with my shoulders twisted to do my job. I couldn't see what was going on in the surgical field.

The patient was shaved bald, and a four-inch square cut opened the scalp. The blood vessels were tied. Next, a stainless steel carpenter's drill and bit drilled four holes in the corners of the exposed scalp. A wire saw was slipped between the holes, and the skull bone that had been measured was removed. Time, thirty minutes.

Deep in the brain is a circular artery called the Circle of Willis. So delicate is the brain that it must be pushed aside by carefully inserting tiny pieces of moist cotton, making sure to keep a count of the number of cotton pieces that were inserted. Total time: two hours and thirty minutes.

The Circle of Willis was found, and a particular arterial branch was to be clamped, which theoretically would help the patient's Parkinson's disease.

The surgeon knew the name but not the location of the branch artery. A nurse was sent to the library for *Gray's Anatomy*. Total time: two hours and fifty minutes.

Clamping the artery: five additional minutes. Total time: two hours and fifty-five minutes.

Removing and counting each piece of cotton one at a time, two hours. Total time: four hours and fifty-five minutes.

Sewing the bone and scalp: thirty-five minutes. Total time: five hours and thirty minutes.

Bored to the point that my mind was screaming, every muscle aching on my twisted body, I fled from the operating theatre when all was completed.

Never again. They would never find me. I hid in broom closets, store rooms anywhere when my name was called to assist. I would have crawled under a bed if I had to. If I was on a posted list, I got sick and went home.

The patient was not the least bit improved by the surgery.

I Killed Her

2:30 am. I AM ALONE on the medical ward of a large New York City hospital. Five rapid admissions arrive. After a quick medical work-up, I know they all need intravenous fluids. I am a master at getting into peoples' veins. When other interns fail, I am called to the rescue. When the needle is inserted into the vein, you allow the fluid to flow in rapidly for a few moments to wash out the blood and avoid clotting.

I would insert the needle, start the rapid flow and go immediately to the next patient. I would insert the needle, start the rapid flow. Then go back to the previous patient to slow the intravenous to a slow, desired rate.

Most of these patients were old, except for one twenty-eight-year-old woman who was in a coma. She had an inoperable brain tumour and had come into the hospital to die. We would have given her minimal attention for two to three months until she was dead.

I forgot to slow down her intravenous drip. The entire bottle flooded her circulation and she went into congestive heart failure. I called for help, but it was of no use – she died. I had killed her.

No one but me knew what had happened, and I kept it that way. Yes, I had been up working with no relief since 8 am the previous day, but I didn't become a doctor to kill anybody. Yes, I just speeded up the inevitable, but I didn't become a doctor to kill anybody. Yes, we were overworked, underpaid and disrespected. But still, I didn't become a doctor to kill anybody.

The hospital administrator told us, "We can do what we want with you. You need your intern certificate or you can't practice medicine. The elevator operator can quit any time, so we have to keep him happy. But we can do what we want with you."

I thought I just felt bad, not guilty, but I told my story to anyone who cared about me and whom I trusted. As I move through time, closer to inevitable death, something has changed. I feel close to her, almost in communion with her.

Screams And Surgery

IT WAS MY FIRST and last surgery. I was an honoured intern being selected to be Chief Surgeon to remove a Bartholin's cyst. Bartholin's glands lubricate the vagina and occasionally enlarge to tennis ball size. Supervised by the head of gynaecological surgery, I made an incision into the depths of the vagina of a 35-year-old white female. Out it came.

You can't see what you are doing when sewing up the vagina. It is all knowledge, sense of feel and experience. Emboldened by having sewn up many postpartum vaginal lacerations, I inserted my curved needle, held at the end of a long hemostat (clamp). The wound was deep so the needle insertion was deep, and hit a pelvic bone. Not a problem, except that the needle broke! I couldn't find it, my consultant couldn't, nor could anyone he called on for help. I was now superfluous and asked to assist at a long operation in another theatre.

I was cool, calm, collected, functioning well and going crazy. In my head I wanted to jump out of a window and land on my head.

The vagina is very vascular. We had not prepared blood for what was to be a short surgery. Oh my God! My first surgery, a disaster. What if she bled to death while they poked around in her vagina just down the hall from me?

As soon as I could, I ran up to our ward. Oh my God! She should have been post operatively in front of the nursing station. She was not. I ran to the one private room at the back of the ward. She was still under anaesthesia but with no supervision. I took her blood pressure. SHE WAS IN SHOCK. There was no help around.

In my best controlled functional hysteria, I ran to the blood bank after taking her blood sample and hollered "Emergency!" I raced with the blood bottle to her room, put it on a stand and into her arm.

I forgot to tie her down.

As she came out of the anaesthesia, she whipped her arm around and knocked the blood bottle over. It smashed on the floor.

Shock, blood all over, panic, and no help. Increasing my level of controlled functional hysteria, I took another blood sample, raced to the blood bank, emergency, ran back to the ward. I tied her down, inserted the blood and slowly lifted her out of shock. She came into consciousness.

As soon as I knew that she was ok, I cleaned up the mess. It was time to go to lunch.

I passed my supervising resident, a gynaecologist in training. He stopped me. "The consultant doesn't blame you. It was his fault. As supervisor, he should have noticed the surgical nurse clamped the needle above the eye, the weak spot. That's why it broke. What bothered him was the way you didn't seem to care!"

I lost it and SCREAMED. "I don't care? I wanted to jump out the window and land on my head, but I had to carry on. I had to function."

Four days later, a military combat team that used a special device designed to locate shrapnel in wounds easily removed the needle.

I hung around my patient's bed from time to time. I felt bad for her and hoped that if I was friendly she wouldn't sue us.

After she left the hospital, she started to send me gifts and love letters and social invitations. A review of her old records showed a social worker report that she was addicted to seducing married men. I slowly and gently cooled her off (in writing).

Yee Haw!

IT WAS JUST ANOTHER DAY on Ward 6B of Queen's General Hospital. Nurses' notes were reviewed. Each patient visited and evaluated. All the IVs started and flowing. The ninety beds on the ward designed for forty were clean and orderly. Each bed was surrounded by curtains suspended from pipes to provide privacy when needed.

The staff, satisfied with their morning's work, strolled to their offices.

Bed 34, a giant black woman with thrombophlebitis began to sing spirituals. Nice voice, never happened before, does no harm.

Suddenly, she leaped up, swung out on the bars like Tarzan, mostly naked in her standard hospital wraparound. She dropped to the ground, bent over and charged down the ward centre aisle shouting, "I am a bull, I am a bull."

The staff fled in terror to the corridor. Only one soul stood his ground – me. I gracefully stepped aside as this unique mad bull charged by.

On her return charge, I leaped on her back and locked her in a full nelson (my arms under her arm pits and around her neck). She collapsed peacefully to the floor. My brave colleagues returned and led her back to bed 34.

She rested in bed for thirty seconds, then leaped up on the pipes and swung her legs out Tarzan style. She almost took the head off my immediate medical superior.

The police arrived with a straitjacket. That calmed her. The men in blue fitted the heavy canvas straitjacket on her and tied her hands behind her back, preparing to take her to the mental hospital.

Suddenly she re-enraged. She flexed her muscles and blasted open the straitjacket seams. Oh my God! She could have killed me!

Harvey R. Wasserman

The Complete Physical

AS SECOND-YEAR medical students on the surgical ward, we were assigned to do complete physical exams on each patient prior to their surgical experience. This was designed to protect the patient and the hospital.

I was assigned to a seventy-five-year-old woman who was to have minor surgery on a wrist tendon the next day.

The physical exam went well until I was about to do a pelvic exam via her vagina. She could not understand what that had to do with a wrist tendon. No amount of explanation seemed to make any sense to her. I finally succeeded, through gentle persuasion, but the experience was most awkward and embarrassing for both of us.

Moment Of Triumph

A YOUNG WOMAN in her twenties was brought to the medical ward in a coma. All the advanced medical staff gathered around and speculated about her diagnosis. It was left to me as a medical intern to do the routine physical while they engaged in their diagnostic speculation.

Reaching across her body to take her blood pressure, I accidentally smelled her breath. Ketones! She was in diabetic ketone acidosis. I quickly obtained a urine sample, ran to the lab and added the reagent that turned blue when there was sugar in the urine.

I returned. In calm triumph I waved the blue tube before my superiors. Disappointed, they drifted away.

I remained, triumphant, and successfully brought her to consciousness.

Harvey R. Wasserman

Olfactory Diagnosis

AS SECOND-YEAR medical students we were directed to smell the vagina of each new mother after childbirth, twice daily. Sounds perverse, but a toxic odour could diagnose a vaginal infection early.

It took a little doing at first to get yourself to practice this brand of medical diagnosis, but the women didn't seem to mind.

There was one exception. A native American Indian lady from a local Indian reservation was always uncomfortable. We found out, and she knew, that her normal healthy vaginal fragrance was three or four times stronger than any Caucasian woman's.

My Entry Into Private Practice

MY FIRST OFFICE had to be beautiful and impressive, large, full of light and many rooms exquisitely decorated with walnut furniture plus a fully equipped playroom so that I could work with young patients.

After I checked everything with the contractor, I was given the front door key the evening before my very first patient was to arrive next morning.

A new suit, white shirt, conservative tie, polished shoes. I arrived early. My key didn't open the front door! I had been given the wrong key! But the office was on the ground floor, and no lock had been placed on the small narrow bathroom window.

I opened the window. Hands first, I was too wide to get in.

In determined desperation I ran at the window, leaped through with my hands clutched at my side, performed a perfect somersault over the toilet bowl, picked myself up, brushed myself off, and opened the front door with the hand-operated inner lock.

In calm dignity I greeted my first patient.

I wrote to a friend who had trained with me describing my entry into practice. He sent it on to the alumni newsletter. My acrobatic initiation became known all over the United States.

A Life Out Of Balance

IN MY FIRST WAITING ROOM was an expensive, exquisite, elegant walnut cocktail table. On the floor were several toys for children who had to wait for their appointment.

My first child patient had been diagnosed as schizophrenic by another psychiatrist. His parents wanted a second opinion.

This five-year-old boy was terrified in my waiting room and refused to enter the bowels of my office and my therapeutic playroom. He took a toy truck and began vigorously denting my exquisite walnut table.

Ignoring his aggression, I calmly started making a tower of blocks from pieces shaped like human beings. He calmed down, came over to watch me. I invited him to help me in my construction. We built the tower and then I told him I had better toys inside.

As he walked in he saw a suction cup dart board and with a charming smile pointed to number five. "That's how old I am." I knew he was not schizophrenic.

On arriving home that very evening I discovered that my youngest son, about four, had made a mess on a stone bench I was building. I screamed at him. *Oh my god, do my children need to pay me like patients for me to treat them with civilised kindness?*

CHAPTER FIFTEEN

FAMILY LIFE

A Fine Christmas Unites the Family
The Wedding Party

A Fine Christmas Unites The Family

ON THE SPUR OF THE MOMENT, I decided to treat my entire family to a classical luxurious Christmas in England. This included myself, my wife, my wife's mother and father, my oldest son, his wife, his newborn child, my radical hippy youngest son and his partner.

What I didn't know was that the Brits love to spend Christmas at a resort. Very little space was available. Our first apartment in London had no heat; my elderly in-laws were freezing. Hours were spent boiling water and filling every receptacle with hot water until the temperature was survivable. We did manage to babysit and send the young parents out for a lovely private dinner.

Then I rented the last Volkswagen minibus in London and drove to Salisbury with its lovely cathedral. We were accepted at an elegant inn but only until the eve before Christmas. The hippy couple had been given a duplex apartment and started to complain about this middle-class luxury with great venom.

Finally, after many phone calls, we found a hotel in the outskirts of London that could house all of us for Christmas and Boxing Day. Hoorah.

On the drive to London, my hippy (sort of) daughter-in-law complained about Christmas without a decorated tree.

Miracle! Christmas Eve we found an open shop with trees and stand and all the decorations. With the Christmas evergreen tied to the Volkswagen roof, we found our hotel. It was built on the site of Henry V's hunting lodge, but it was really an old folk's retirement home with rooms to rent for visiting relatives. What could we do? It was room and board, but what about the tree? Would it be allowed? We decided to take no chances.

The dining room had a reinforced glass roof just under our sleeping quarters on the third floor. We lifted my hippy son to

Harvey R. Wasserman

the dining room roof, hoping no one would look up, and low-ered a rope from the third floor window. Handing the tree up to the dining room roof and tying it to the rope, we sneaked our eight-foot tree into the apartment and joyfully decorated it. To add to the picturesque experience, at each meal my hippy son dressed with increased casual sloppiness, even seeming a bit dirtier.

While we were down with Santa in the entrance way, my wife locked herself out of her room, wearing only a see-through dressing gown. To get a key she had no alternative but to take the elevator to the lobby. "Oh my gracious!" was the formal group response of the very proper British to her arrival.

And so another family Christmas retreats into memory.

The Wedding Party

MY YOUNGER SON was born an intense, passionate, left-wing radical. He and his partner settled in America's largest commune, "The Farm," in Tennessee. At its peak, ten thousand middle-class young people were there, rebelling against the system.

I visited several times and have two outstanding memories. One memory was youngsters coming up to me. "Are you a grandfather?" they said with wonder and sparkle in their eyes. I admitted that I was the rare exotic creature that they had identified.

The Farm specialised in natural childbirth, publishing books including ones about natural childbirth, doing actual natural childbirth, music and some farming. What was wondrous to me were the food and clothing tents.

These great tents contained food and clothing. But no one stood watch; no one supervised.

In the first tent, each type of vegetarian food had a sign: "Plenty of this, take all you need," or "This is limited in supply, one carton full for each person." In the clothing tent, clothes were arranged by sex and size, all washed, pressed and in good repair. You took what you needed, no signs. I felt an incredible sense of peace in both tents.

One August my wife and I flew to a small town in North Carolina to negotiate the purchase of beautiful piece of rural property. The Farm was not that far away, which gave us a chance to see my son and his partner. I arranged a rental car for them. They arrived at 10 am. We were to leave for Peru via Miami at 3:30 pm.

She was pregnant! No problem for me. The Farm didn't care if you were married. My son and his partner had frequently proclaimed their belief that with commitment, legal marriage was irrelevant.

Harvey R. Wasserman

Unknown to me, my wife didn't relish having an illegitimate grandchild. Unknown to me she and my son's partner in quiet consultation discovered that my son's partner really wanted to be married before childbirth. They came speaking pleasantly and presented the desire for marriage to my son. To my astonished surprise, he agreed.

First we needed his birth certificate for the approval of the Chief of the City Council so the proper forms could be issued. My wife confronted the official: "I gave birth to him. I ought to know where and when he was born." The certificate was issued. Fortunately, the official didn't seem to remember that he needed a birth certificate from my son's partner. That was just ignored.

Second, the bride and groom needed a medical exam. An emergency call to a local physician brought an appropriate response.

Third, a venereal disease blood test was a state requirement. The local hospital laboratory only did it on Tuesdays. Hurrah! It was Tuesday.

On arriving at the hospital with the blood samples, we were informed, "The lab only does marital blood on Tuesday until 12 pm." I had arrived at 12:30.

"Sorry!"

I pleaded; no result. I flaunted my MD and professorship at Yale. No result. I tried significant money bribery. No result.

I broke down and cried. The lab gave up their lunch hour. The result was blood tests and joyous thanks.

Fourth, we needed a person who could legally create a marriage. A Justice of the Peace was located and committed to a 1 pm service in her office.

In the meantime, I made or received six to ten phone calls about the land deal. Hurrah! An agreement was reached.

I needed to leave goodwill money to seal the land deal. This required a trip to the local bank, where I unknowingly left my wallet. Some very honest citizen found it, tracked me down and returned it to me. I didn't even know I had lost it.

My future daughter-in-law called her mother on an outside public phone to tell her about the impending marriage. "Go on, get married, see if I care!"

My future daughter-in-law collapsed to the ground. I revived her with a glass of water.

On to the office of the lovely female Justice of the Peace with the most profound Southern accent I have ever encountered. I most remember one comment of hers as part of the ceremony: EYE DEE WIDTH OL MAH WORLDLEGH GOOTZ DOOTH INDOWE.

"What?" exclaimed my son.

Before he could protest further, I translated. "I thee with all my worldly goods doth endow."

"Yes."

Hugs and kisses followed, ending with my son announcing he had lost the keys to the rental car. On to the local car agency. They took the front left door apart, found the code and made a key.

The happy bridal pair promptly demanded a wedding party. Off to the local supermarket to buy any vegetarian goodies we could find and a gallon of milk.

Back to the motel and a hasty, happy, vegetarian wedding gluttony.

The police knew what the situation was. They rushed us to the airport, where a waiting motorised cart made a mad dash for the flight gate.

With thirty seconds to spare, we were on our way to Peru and vacation.

A lovely little granddaughter was born five months later.

CHAPTER SIXTEEN

ONCE IN A LIFETIME THERAPY

Lewd Phone Call Therapy
The Power Of Pleasure Bonding
Misdirected Terror
Hit In The Head Therapy
Milton Erickson
Third-Eye Communion
Hellmuth Kaiser
Groucho Marx And The Nude Encounter Group

Lewd Phone Call Therapy

MARRIAGES are more likely to deteriorate than to blossom.

The American couple was no exception to this probability. They barely spoke, much less communicated, had frequent rows, plenty of emotional pain and anger. The one exception was that they shared the same marital bed. There was no other place to sleep!

I worked with them professionally for two visits without much happening. But that third visit!

They walked into my office and leered at me with a strange look of bemusement. They both said, several times, "That was some phone call, Harvey."

I ran through my memory bank. I hadn't called them since our last appointment.

"We knew you were a bit unusual. Your phone call was certainly most unusual."

This went on for a while, accompanied by smiling, salacious, smirking expressions. I finally couldn't stand their strange behaviour, and I was finally certain I had never called them.

"I never called you."

On her side of the bed was the telephone. Just after they retired for the night, the phone rang. She picked it up. Thinking it was my voice, she listened to a long dirty phone call. She became very excited and seduced her husband. He responded enthusiastically. For the first time in years, they pleasure bonded. The door of pain, anger and self-protection opened.

From then on, my therapy in the office worked beautifully.

The Power Of Pleasure Bonding

CINDY WAS A SAD, unhappy, depressed, 42-year-old house-wife. "He never touches or hugs me. He never buys me a present, doesn't believe in them. There is plenty of money. He won't give me any to recover the living room furniture. My home is important to me."

Bill, her husband, was a highly technical research scientist devoted to his work.

Out of my mouth came a suggestion to Cindy that I was never taught, never thought of and a surprise to me. Where did it come from?

"Could you seduce him every night?" comfortably rolled out of my vocal cords.

"Yes I can," she replied.

I have never offered such a suggestion before or since and probably never will. Most women would say no.

Two weeks later, she entered my office looking ten years younger. Cindy was happy, even bubbly, not a sign of sadness or depression.

"Everything has changed. He came home in the middle of the week with a bunch of roses. He gave me money to recover the living room furniture. I get kissed and hugged. Most remarkable of all, he bought a whole outfit of clothes. He never buys new clothes."

Six weeks later she entered my office looking happy and bubbly.

"Last night he took me aside and told me, 'Could you please slow down? I am getting older, and I can't keep up with you.' "

(And they lived happily ever after.)

Misdirected Terror

"I AM TERRIFIED!" exclaimed Mary as she moved into my patient chair.

"I can't sleep, I can't concentrate, or work. I am shaking all over. It makes no sense. I am scheduled for minor day hospital surgery on one of my left wrist tendons. I know the risk is negligible, but I am convinced that I will die. I think incessantly of dying from the surgery. I can't stop these thoughts. I know they make no sense, but that changes nothing."

It made no sense to me either. A complete history discovered no previous trauma that might have been reactivated. Was there a buried wish to die? No luck there either! Hypnosis, nothing! Working with other emotions – nothing. Everything I tried to bring light to her terror of death was fruitless.

I finally asked her to visualise the hospital, the surgery and her death. She willingly accomplished this task. I then suggested that she imagine her spirit leaving her body and in the distance see a bright light. "Follow the light to the tunnel of light. Enter the tunnel and follow it to the end where you will be greeted."

There was brief silence as her imagination entered and moved through the tunnel.

Suddenly she screamed, "All my dead relatives are there!" Still screaming, "I hate them! I never want to be with them again. I'm not afraid of dying; I'm terrified of being with them again."

Opening her eyes, "My terror is gone." She was at peace and remained terror free. Her surgery became a minor event.

Harvey R. Wasserman

Hit In The Head Therapy

DORIS WAS a 38-year-old married professor of psychology at a prestigious university. She had been in psychoanalytic therapy for many years with no results. Finally she showed up at my office.

The beginning of therapy with this intelligent, lively woman was interesting but didn't seem to change very much. Until one day she entered my office and announced, "I feel I am a rat." I invited her to get down on all fours and be her rat.

She got down on all fours and became her rat. She crawled around my office for some time, examining and sniffing every piece of furniture she came in contact with. Gradually, she approached me in my chair. Carefully sniffing my leg, she bit me a mighty bite! Not a love bite – it hurt for three days.

I reacted automatically with no thought in my head. I hit her in the head with my open right hand and sent her flying across the room. With exceptional good luck, she landed on a couch. My unconscious must have been in some control, as my hand was open and not a fist. I apparently shoved her and did not hurt her.

She screamed, "You hit me!"

"You bit me!"

"You encouraged me to be spontaneous and look what happened!"

"I never said there wouldn't be consequences."

Therapy became deep, profound, trusting and rapid. In six months we accomplished what eight years of previous therapy had failed to produce.

Milton Erickson

MESMER, the first great and famous hypnotherapist (mesmerism) in the 18th century may have been reincarnated in the life of Milton Erickson. Most dedicated hypnotherapists worship at the sound of his name.

One of my professional friends organised a two-and-half day workshop with Milton. I was very excited, since I had heard many complimentary stories about him.

What I experienced instead was world class boredom. I spent my time practising landing imaginary airplanes, just as I had done during boring lectures in medical school. I was going to quit and head home, but my friends put pressure on me to stay. Instead, I decided to confront Milton. He was hard to be aggressive with. Milton was charming, confined to a wheelchair, one arm paralysed and slightly distorted in his speech. Still I tried.

"Milton, I came here to learn about hypnotherapy, and I haven't learned anything about hypnotherapy."

Milton: "What makes you think you are not hypnotised right now?"

Me: "What makes me think I am hypnotised?"

There was no reply.

"Milton, you are very famous – I would like to be famous, and I am not. How can I become famous like you?"

Milton: "Be very good at what you do."

Me: "I am already very good at what I do, and I am not famous."

Milton: no reply.

Some of my friends thought that something important had happened to me at the workshop with Erickson, because unlike my usual behaviour, I kept complaining about it for months after the workshop was over, and even got headaches when I talked about it.

Five months later I went through the most creative period of my life. Every day new ideas appeared to me. Some of the new ideas were based on previous work of mine. Other ideas came from nowhere. They all worked. This joyous time lasted eight months and then without explanation stopped.

The eight months were wonderful, better than money or sex and resulted in what I call the five spiritual energies. I fought writing the five spiritual energies down for one whole day, then succumbed at 11 pm and put them to paper. I showed the writing of my five spiritual energies to Dr. Russ Jaffee, my teacher of Chinese Medicine. He shocked me. "You have rediscovered the healing secrets of Atlantis."

Later that year I was presenting some new ideas at an IHLRN workshop. One member, a PhD psychologist, was fascinated. After the workshop she wanted to learn more about it. I obliged her wish and then told her the story of the rise and fall of those many months of creativity. She told me to think about everything I had studied, every workshop I had attended during the six months before the period of creativity. I had been going to workshops for almost every weekend. I reviewed them silently in my mind. When I came to Milton, she screamed, "THAT'S IT! THAT'S IT!" I tested her three more times by reviewing my experiences. When I came to Milton, she screamed, "THAT'S IT! THAT'S IT!"

Milton had died by then, so I acquired some of his videotapes. I watched them each evening before bedtime and was, as usual with Milton, bored out of my mind before I went to bed. After a few weeks my creativity increased but not at the frequency or uniqueness as it had when I worked with Milton.

I had further contact with the Mexican PhD psychotherapist and happened to mention to her what Dr. Russ Jaffee had said, to which she replied, "Harvey, every night when I go to sleep I go to Atlantis, and you are always there."

As I continued to listen to Milton's tapes, I noticed that he was doing something to my consciousness through the videotape and finally I was able to do it myself. I call it producing a state of communion in another person, a feeling of safety and peace without a word being said. I have not only produced this state with individuals, but with large audiences successfully.

When a person acknowledges that they can sense their change in consciousness, I tell them to move around in their minds and do the same thing to me. I can tell when they are close, and then encourage them to continue until I sense they are spot on. I then ask them to do it to me as I do it to them. The effect is lovely.

Clinically, I deliberately create this state with shy and distrusting patients. It works with most people, but a few will not react to it.

All the outstanding therapists that I supervise immediately produce this state when they present a patient they are having trouble with. They do not know that they are doing it until I teach them how to do it consciously with me.

My friend John Kessler, a professor of physics, can do it better and stronger than I can. He can walk through a group of wild rattlesnakes and laugh. They don't attack him. They know he is not dangerous.

Reports have reached me that zoo-based gorillas also respond.

I have never tried to teach this in writing, but here goes:

Soften your vision, your eyes very slightly out of focus and imagine they are looking out of your third eye, which is about a one-half to three-quarters of an inch above the area between your eyebrows. Place your mind in a benevolent state, temporarily without any thoughts. Let me know if this works for you.

Third-Eye Communion

WHEN TOUCHING IS APPROPRIATE, communion can be achieved by massaging firmly and smoothing between your partner's eyebrows. Stroke upward for one inch with your thumb.

At the top of the stroke, lift your thumb and bring it down to the starting point between the eyebrows. Repeat five or six times or until you can sense your partner's relaxed state of consciousness. Thumb pressure should be firm but not painful.

Now have your partner repeat the same third-eye stroking with you. Make certain the stroking is not too fast, a common fault.

When you sense your consciousness shift, suggest that you do it to each other simultaneously. In five to ten strokes, both of you should feel relaxed, safe and in deep communion with each other in the absence of words.

Several species of reptiles have a third eye with a retina that joins its brain where our pineal gland is located. In addition to its hormonal production, our pineal gland is richly connected to many parts of the brain, function unclear.

Hellmuth Kaiser — I Treasure Everything He Ever Taught Me

HELLMUTH KAISER was born after World War I, of German academics. During the Great Depression, he became a successful industrialist. Unfulfilled by business success, he became depressed. His depression led him to try psychoanalysis. On completing psychoanalytic treatment, he was rejected by the German Psychoanalytic Society. Only physicians were admitted to the German Psychoanalytic Society.

Hellmuth published a brilliant psychoanalytic interpretation of Hamlet. This so impressed Freud that Freud personally bent the rules and brought Hellmuth into the German Psychoanalytic Society.

Over a period of time he began to doubt the effectiveness of psychoanalytic therapy. His work became profoundly influenced through a seminar on character analysis with Wilhelm Reich. This experience started him on his own highly effective path.

I worked with Hellmuth personally in therapy and supervision for one year, after my three years of training at the Menninger School of Psychiatry, where the focus was on the psychoanalytic psychotherapy. My year with Hellmuth profoundly influenced my own growth and my success with patients.

Hellmuth's ideas sound simple but are powerful when applied:

1. THE UNIVERSAL HUMAN PATHOLOGY, which he called The Illusion Of Fusion. The desire to surrender your individuality by merging with another person, a group, or an ideology. This concept explains a vast amount of human behaviour. Think about suicide bombers, synchronised swimming, marriage, and what is known as the herd mentality.

Harvey R. Wasserman

2. THE UNIVERSAL SYMPTOM – Duplicity. This is a disharmony between body, speech, attitudes and behaviour. A simple example is someone who proclaims their peacefulness of mind, while vigorously tapping their foot.

3. THE UNIVERSAL THERAPY — Clear, Honest, Non-Judgemental Communication. Take a look at Chapter 6, the section on the Lama Govinda, for someone who has achieved clear, integrated, coherent communication.

Groucho Marx And The Nude Encounter Group

ONLY GROUCHO could have imagined this weekend, and it really happened.

My wife and I had attended a "peak experience" workshop conducted by psychologist Paul Bindrim. Favourite smells, tastes, touch, music, breathing exercises, produced an interesting altered state of consciousness. As "peak experience" ended, Paul invited us to attend his nude encounter group at a nudist colony in New Jersey. My wife wasn't interested. I was.

As we paid our fee we signed a "non-fucking agreement" for the duration of the workshop. The consequences of any violation of such a solemn agreement were not made clear.

As we assembled, fully clothed, in a large meeting room, Paul whispered to me, "Harvey if you want to work with anyone, feel free to do so".

WHAT?

Paul hardly knew me. I came to participate. I had worked all week with patients. I had paid my money.

There were at least forty participants. In hindsight, there were many more than he could handle.

Picture a large circle of clothed seated participants being asked one by one if they had any problem taking off all their clothes. This began after Paul announced that he had a stiff neck from fucking with some lady while standing on their heads the day before the workshop.

Most denied any problem with nudity except for a select few.

"Yes – I am afraid the females will reject me because my penis is too small."

He was instructed to take off his clothes and ask each woman one by one if they would reject him with a small penis.

They all compassionately replied, "No." Paul then had him ask the men until one said "I can't afford to reject you; my penis so small."

This always happened. Paul was prepared. He whipped out a ruler and invited any male concerned about his penis size to strip and enter the smallest penis contest. There were eight volunteers who stripped. They were carefully measured. The winner with the smallest penis was declared (I don't remember his measurement) and vigorously cheered and applauded by the group. The winner was very pleased to have won.

The next volunteer to admit discomfort in public disrobing was an attractive, well-built woman about thirty-five years of age. "I am afraid the men will reject me because my breast is scarred since I had a baby." Off came her clothes, revealing a lovely body. Her breasts were large with a remarkably youthful shape. You would need a magnifying glass to observe the minute scar caused by stretch marks from her pregnancy. All the men gallantly admired her breasts and assured her that their only reaction was positive. She seemed particularly interested in my favourable reaction to her bosom and its insignificant scar.

The last participant to declare his discomfort was male. "I know the men and women will reject me because I only have one ball." Off came his clothes and a tour of the group. "Do you reject me because I only have one ball?" The answers were mostly "No, of course not." As a matter of fact, when a male is born with a single testicle, the other enlarges and it is almost impossible to tell the difference. One enthusiastic female replied, "When you make love to a man, who counts?"

"I can't afford to reject you," came one intense male reply.

"WHY NOT!!"

"Because I only have one ball myself." Now both men exposed themselves together to the rest of the group, all of whom denied any inclination to reject them.

It was now time for total group nudity. As we left the meeting room for the body temperature pool, I remarked to Paul, "This ball thing must have happened before."

"No, never. Not one single testicle, much less two single testicles, in the workshops I have presented."

We then submerged our nudity in a big body temperature pool that had been tarted up with underwater coloured lights and sound system. We took turns floating on our backs, held up in the water by a pair of participants facing each other with outstretched arms, passing us from one couple to another couple, the length of the pool. The effect was pleasantly sensual, deeply relaxing, even light trance inducing. Then it was staggering to bed time in one large room. We slept for four hours on sleeping bags we brought with us. That was Friday night and Saturday morning.

The explosion, the action, took place back in the pool starting early Saturday morning. People started "primaling" after the fashion and writing of Dr. Arthur Janov. Dr. Janov's therapy was to put people into early states of consciousness and have them scream whatever was bothering them at the time.

We certainly had screaming, crying, vomiting, "Daddy!", "Mummy!" flailing about, falling on their backs. At first only one person at a time "primaled." Paul did a very simple body therapy. He floated them on their backs and pressed on their chests with both hands to keep them breathing and discharging their emotions. Paul balanced on one foot, the other knee raised to support the primaler's back so they would not drown. At the same time, the lady with the minute breast scar kept following me around the pool so she could stand with our bodies touching. I swam away to the other side of the pool, only to be followed. I crossed the pool many times.

Suddenly more and more people started primaling. Paul couldn't handle them all. At times it took five to six minutes before the primaling settled down. The group became upset and didn't know what to do, and THEN everyone looked at me. I didn't come to work. I came to participate and observe. I swam away several times. Finally I couldn't resist the group pressure or the distress of the primalers. Balancing on one foot in the water with the other raised to support your patient is not easy, and you have to press hard on their chest with two hands and keep the process moving.

The first "patient" that the group brought to me was a beautiful young woman with beautiful large breasts. I did my duty with slight hesitation at first. I pressed on her breasts. I pressed away to keep her bellowing and kept her crying, "Mammy." Suddenly I broke out laughing. At the time I was a professor at the Yale University College of Medicine, Department of Psychiatry. While pressing on her breasts, I fantasised there was a hidden video camera somewhere in the pool. The video would be shown at the Department of Psychiatry grand rounds next Wednesday, with the entire faculty in attendance. How could I help but laugh?

I was co-therapist with Paul for the remainder of the day and evening. Next morning the CLIMAX! Paul himself fell on his back, thrashing about and making groaning sounds. Everyone looked at me. What could I do? I started treating the teacher.

Paul was a major challenge, groaning and yelling and kicking. I balanced on my right foot, left knee supporting his back. Paul was incredibly strong. His kicking propelled us like a ten horsepower motor. No standing in one place and working. We were propelled backward. I found myself hopping rapidly on one foot, hoping I could keep up and keep us from going under water. Finally he "de-primaled." I don't know how long it took. It seemed to me a very long time.

As he returned to normal consciousness, the group gathered around him.

"This must have happened to you before."

"No, never."

"Why now?"

"There never was anybody I thought could take care of me."

Then dressing. There followed a short group summary meeting. I noticed the group surrounded and complimented Paul and ignored and isolated me. They didn't know what to do with me. No one came all that distance and paid all that money to see what I could do.

I felt deeply pleased and contented. As we finished, no one spoke to me except the lady with the invisible scar on her left bosom. She invited me to meet her at a nearby motel. I politely declined.

It was an hour and a half drive home. I laughed all the way. The brief intrusive thought that I deserved a refund was pushed aside. I was fully repaid with laughter and a unique memory.

CHAPTER SEVENTEEN

THE FIVE SPIRITUAL ENERGIES

The Five Spiritual Energies

The Five Spiritual Energies

ENERGY LEVEL I: The Physical Level

AURIC COLOUR: Lavender

PSYCHOLOGICAL CHARACTERISTICS: The ability to say no in any situation; to clearly know what one believes, wants, and knows; to interact with the environment in a lively, passionate manner. A person in a high state of this energy would be called a centred and grounded person with a good sense of "I-ness."

PHYSICAL LEVEL INTERSECTS: The energy at this level is a boundary energy that should exist at every point that the individual interacts with and encounters the outside world. This energy is particularly focused in the legs, where the contact with the earth is of prime importance, in the pelvis and there involved in sexual contact, and the head, especially the eyes in making visual contact with the world. (Eyes have a contact as well as a visual function.)

PHYSICAL STIMULATION: This energy can be enhanced by slow, sensual rotary motions of all parts of the body. The most essential areas of rotation are starting individually with each ankle, then go to the knees and then go to the hip joints. [Make certain that each rotation is unusually slow. This requires concentration. Fast rotation is more natural but ineffective. Slow enough rotation is confirmed by an increase of bodily warmth and a pleasant sensation in the joint being rotated. Make certain that each joint is stimulated without rotating the other joints.] The energy is also stimulated by initially gently massaging of the heart chakra point on the foot (to the side and below the inner side of the pad of the big toe).

MEDITATION: I passionately encounter the world.

PSYCHOPATHOLOGY: Ungroundedness, flatness, fearfulness, usually from early pathological bonding between mother and child.

ENERGY LEVEL II: The Emotional Level

AURIC COLOUR: Pink

PSYCHOLOGICAL CHARACTERISTICS: Self-love and self-esteem

PHYSICAL LEVEL: Intersects primarily at the level of the spine and around the spine from the upper lumbar area to the mid-thoracic area in back of the heart. Also the mid-sternal area of the front of the chest.

PHYSICAL MEDITATION AND STIMULATION: With your body horizontal, knees bent, rotate the pelvis downward while breathing in, and then on exhalation slowly lift the pelvis so that each spinal section is lifted individually up to the top area of the heart in the mid-thoracic region. Continue for about five minutes.

MEDITATION: I was born to love myself.

PSYCHOPATHOLOGY: This energy is inhibited by any creation of self-doubt or self-negation as a child, but very powerfully when a child is born not wanted, when a child is born of a sex different than the parents wish. In such cases anxiety, not self-esteem, is the result and should be treated by angrily attacking this profound rejection. It is possible that such influences start in utero, long before birth.

ENERGY LEVEL III: The Astral Level

AURIC COLOUR: Golden Yellow

PSYCHOLOGICAL CHARACTERISTICS: When a person is in a highly charged state with this energy, their characteristics are much like the thinking of an innocent but not naïve child who means well to himself and to all the world. In such a state it is impossible to be spiteful or negativistic to any human being or any living creature. In addition, in this state when fully developed, there is a sense of being connected with a much larger and greater benevolence that might be called God.

PHYSICAL LEVEL INTERSECTS: This energy is contained within the abdomen, possibly related to the solar plexus. It is contained by spasm and tightness in the abdominal muscles, the muscles of the pelvic floor and the diaphragm.

PHYSICAL MEDITATION AND STIMULATION: This energy can be released temporarily by breathing in a broken staccato manner on both inhalation and exhalation. On inhalation, the abdominal muscles and the pelvic floor are tightened as well. There is a brief pause at the end of inhalation, and then about halfway through staccato exhalation the abdominal muscles and pelvic floor are relaxed as profoundly as possible. Both the abdominal and the pelvic floor are then pushed out. Done properly, only three or four breaths are necessary to release this energy.

MEDITATION: Innocent benevolent thought brings us home within the house of God.

PSYCHOPATHOLOGY: When a child's innocent benevolence is treated cruelly and insensitively, leading to a constricted, limited and/or materialistic life.

ENERGY LEVEL IV: The Etheric Level

AURIC COLOUR: White, a pearlescent white

PSYCHOLOGICAL CHARACTERISTICS: In a high state of this energy, a person feels energetic, is in a happy mood. There are frequent outbursts of laughter, often with minimal or no stimulation. The laughter has an infectious quality and seems to originate more from the belly than the chest. There is an accepting and humorous understanding of the paradox of your own and other people's existence that can be verbalised as, "Everybody else seems very foolish, almost as foolish as I find myself to be." This state is also accompanied by a profound level of self-acceptance. Sentences that are appropriate to this energy state are, "Everything I worry about is silly; my laughter shows the power; I accept myself at the profoundest level."

PHYSICAL LEVEL OF INTERACTION: The first and second chakra areas, the sixth and seventh chakra areas, and probably the whole spinal column.

PHYSICAL MEDITATION AND STIMULATION: Brought about by rolling a small blanket roll and putting it in the lower small of the back, knees bent, and then rapidly rolling the pelvis up and down over the blanket roll, coordinated with breathing as follows: when the pelvis goes down, breathing in; when the pelvis goes up, breathing out. Hands stretched out straight over the head. This causes a rapid, undulating action over the whole spinal column. It is also important to precede or accompany this physical exercise by a mental image in which one breathes in and fantasizes while breathing in that the air is coming in through the sixth and seventh chakras and moving down the front of the body to the perineal area, and on breathing out rises up the back along the spinal column to emerge again from the sixth and seventh chakra.

MEDITATION: My laughter shows / brings the power.

ENERGY LEVEL V: The Mental Level

AURIC COLOUR: Golden Green. This colour has been described as the colour of the early morning sunlight coming through new wheat, or indirect sunlight coming through a full bottle of Tanqueray gin.

PSYCHOLOGICAL CHARACTERISTICS: In this energy state, a person is knowing, as well as able to think clearly in a manner that could be called wisdom, wisdom perhaps being defined as knowing replacing fear. This energy has the quality of healing both on a psychological and physical level.

PHYSICAL LEVEL INTERSECTS: The back of the head starting in the area near the posterior fontanelle, the back of the neck and upper shoulders.

PHYSICAL MEDITATION AND STIMULATION: Visualising a lovely Kelly green light with golden sunlight warming the areas of physical intersect. If doing laying on of hands healing, picture this light streaming down the arms into the hands.

MEDITATION: Perfect wisdom heals us / me.

PSYCHOPATHOLOGY: Any illness, physical or mental that is part of our being cut off from our essential truths, our spiritual essence and values and from the divine cosmic unity.

CHAPTER EIGHTEEN

CHARACTER DEFECTS

Love Phobia
Self-Pity
I Won't Know Who I Am
"I Want" Deficiency
Goodbye Self-Torture, The Ego-Alien Technique
Temporal Tapping
Self-Hypnosis To Intensify Temporal Tapping

Love Phobia

I AM A LOVE PHOBE and damn reluctant to admit it.

Shortly after my marriage, my wife complained about a cycle of friendship, love and intimacy followed by my picking a fight. Of course, I denied it. After two to three years of her repetition, I paid attention. I realised she was accurate. Love, intimacy, pick a fight, make up and repeat the cycle. What the hell was going on? It made no sense. All I could do at first was to apologise and take a walk when I sensed my destructive impulse. One day I sensed fear behind my irritability. At least I could confess my fear before I took my walk.

My mother was very subtly controlling. I was a mama's boy. If I had given her all my heart, there would have been nothing left of me. When the critical point was reached, the silent alarm went off and closed my heart. I had to begin to face my fear of allowing myself to be controlled in the warmth of intimacy.

"Something is wrong with me," announced a bright, good-looking twenty-eight-year-old man as he settled into my patient chair. "In eight relationships I have fallen in love. After a while I have my doubts, get negative, and withdraw. When my woman responds by backing off in self-protection, I can feel my love for her again. Eventually, either she or I can't stand it and we break up. The woman I love the most has started to appear on television. Every time I see her, I am aware of what I destroyed. I become miserable. What is wrong with me?"

For a time, almost every other week a man would consult me with the same story.

If I could help them sense the fear, there was hope. The focus was then on the fear. What were they afraid of – being hurt, being rejected, being controlled, being abandoned, surrendering oneself totally to another human being?

More urgent was the fear that if my patient's partner betrayed him, he would unleash his rage and kill her.

Harvey R. Wasserman

When the fear is acknowledged in the relationship and worked on in psychotherapy, the results are promising. When fear cannot be acknowledged, the results are dismal.

A brief article about this tragic phenomenon appeared in a local paper. Mothers started referring their daughters.

One of the more dramatic examples was a young man who broke off with his partner when he temporarily went abroad for specialised training. One week later he emailed me, "I am madly in love with her. Am I crazy?"

"No, you are a love phobe."

On his return he tried to reconnect, but she'd had enough.

When love is so vital to any meaningful life, why does it also expose so many of us to real or imagined great danger? Can anyone make sense of this to me on a spiritual or a Darwinian level?

I have found *The Heart Roots Exercise* (Chapter 11) very helpful to love phobes and people with emotionally damaged hearts. (Also see *Devastation or Healing, Emotional Pain*, Chapter 12)

Self-Pity

SELF-PITY IS AS FREQUENT and often as debilitating as depression. It is rarely discussed in lay or professional literature.

Self-pity has none of the side effects of depression but it is as effective as depression in preventing constructive and effective action. Self-pity is saying to yourself and to the world, "It shouldn't have happened. It shouldn't be happening to me. I am going to sit here and not move until someone eliminates whatever shouldn't have happened."

You have created a massively immature inner child.

Self-pity has another unique component. Self-pitying thoughts are extremely and often persistently attractive to the self-pitier. But when you hear a self-pitier, you are almost universally repulsed.

How do you know if you are in a self-pitying state? Does your mind stay preoccupied with the undesirable event and avoid corrective actions and attitudes, even though they may occasionally creep into consciousness?

There is also an element of self-righteous indignation that is usually observable. In self-pity there is suffering, but it is less severe than in most depression. The suffering is complained about but readily tolerated.

How do you detect that you are in this state?

Noting that you stay preoccupied with the undesirable event and not corrective action is one way. Saying "poor me" before you recount your personal victimisation can shift the emotional anaesthesia of self-pity.

If you have the courage, ask a close, honest, equally courageous friend, "Do I sound like I am in self-pity?"

Harvey R. Wasserman

The intellectual awareness that self-pity promotes paralysis, disrespect, low self-esteem and unhappiness, can at times launch you into a healthier mental state.

The best way I have found to treat self-pity is to have the patient exaggerate and even clown "poor me" and to continue exaggerating while they state in detail their complaint against the disharmony in their life. If they laugh as they do this, they are on their way to health.

It is important that they not fall into a subsequent trap of self-condemnation. They have faced their situation courageously.

In any therapy, I introduce self-pity awareness by asking my patient (as good naturedly as possible), "Would you say you are in a state of self-pity?" They almost always say yes and smile. A crack in the door toward healing is opened.

I Won't Know Who I Am

"I AM AFRAID of almost everything in life!"

Marge is a very intelligent woman about 40 years of age. She is slightly plump but makes a very pleasant appearance. She had tried many therapists with no result. She relied on her parents for all decisions, couldn't drive a car. Her husband ordered her around and showed her no respect.

As with all new patients, I wanted to give her hope on her first visit. I asked permission to massage certain acupressure points on her body. Halfway down her body, she shouted "STOP!"

"Why do you want me to stop?"

"My fear is going away!"

"That's the general idea. Why do you want me to stop?"

"I WON'T KNOW WHO I AM!"

Oh my God, she identified herself with her fear.

Using the ego-alien technique, which can be examined in this chapter, and other approaches, Marge started to strike out for herself, away from her parents and husband.

They counterattacked and demanded that she remain her former self.

Not yet strong enough and afraid of being abandoned, she surrendered.

If you are about to make an important change in your beliefs or behaviour and think "I won't know who I am," be assured that you are about to discover who you are. Tolerate the temporary emptiness and anxiety.

Harvey R. Wasserman

"I-Want" Deficiency - Passion Suppressed

PASSION IS THE VIGOUR, the intensity with which we contact the world.

Sexual passion is central. But sex is only one way to contact the environment. Passion belongs in the eyes, taking in all that can be seen — a beautiful sunset or even a squalid part of your city. Passion belongs in your skin, especially your fingers, the pleasure of touching skin or of stroking fine silk or velvet. Passion belongs in your feet and legs as you move and contact the earth beneath you. Passion belongs in your breath as you inhale and react to the air and the aromas you breathe in. Passion belongs in your mouth as you identify the flavours you put against your tongue.

Every child is born passionate. Every child wants to be cleaned, to be touched, fondled and cuddled, to be fed, loved, spoken to and played with. When the baby doesn't get these essentials, it screams passionately (we call it crying), demanding what it expects. As a child gets older, it passionately wants everything that attracts its attention and feels passionately entitled to it. In the terrible twos, a child passionately stakes his right to his separateness and individuality by saying no, the basic expression of independence.

The universal "want" of the developing child must be civilised. When this is too vigorously curtailed, passion begins to wither. When the "no" fight for selfhood is too vigorously suppressed, passion continues to be weakened, even to die. The rigorous control of the child's sense of direction may produce direction for a while, but it ends in the collapse of passion.

Passion cannot be imposed from the outside. A passionless person doesn't know what they want in life and has no sense of direction. Extremely intelligent people will end up stuck in menial jobs. Ask such a person, "What do you want to do or to be in your life?" The answer is inevitably, "I don't know."

The passion we are born with is part of our life force. Passion is necessary for getting what you want. As you reach for what you want, there are always obstacles. With passion you can go through under, over or around the obstacles. The path out of "I-want deficiency" is not usually quick or easy because the suppression of passion occurs early in life and is profoundly crippling.

Passion healing can be practised at home or in your office.

1. Express anger at being robbed of your passion.

2. Have a temper tantrum and yell from the belly, "No!"

3. Have a temper tantrum and yell from the belly, "I want it!"

4. Find a dish towel and trap it in a closed door. The other end of the towel is held in the back teeth so that the front teeth are not compromised. Pull at the towel with your mouth, your entire body behind it. Growl like a dog protecting its bone.

5. Notice everything that has appeal as you pass through the day and try to feel, "I want it;" "I deserve it;" "It's mine."

Write and meditate, "I passionately encounter the world." Imagine these words are imprinted in your brain, your throat, your heart, your belly.

(See *The "No" Cure of Dyspareunia*, Chapter 8.)

Goodbye Self-Torture, The Ego-Alien Technique

MOST PEOPLE call themselves nasty names when they make a mistake. Some people even believe that being nasty to yourself is a good thing to do. It isn't. Self-judge-mentalness promotes low self-esteem and depression. The steps to healing are simple in concept:

Step 1: Awareness of the problem.

Step 2: Awareness of the problem without judge-mentalness. We rarely choose the limitations and miseries that we immerse ourselves in.

Step 3: Do whatever you can to limit and control your negativity.

Step 4: Do whatever you can to cure the limitations of self-torture we are so devoted to.

Beginning private practice is scary for everyone. Fear was not the problem for me. If I worked with eight patients, it only took one that I judged to be inadequately treated to send me home miserable (depressed). This made no sense. The only way to be perfect is to be perfectly dead. It made more sense to learn from the one person that I didn't handle as well as I would have liked to.

I began to visualise my self-torture as a foreign body and gave it the name SELF-TORTURER.

Fighting with SELF-TORTURER caused more torture.

Speaking to SELF-TORTURER in a polite and slightly positive manner was highly effective. SELF-TORTURER was like a neighbour that I wouldn't invite for a cup of coffee but would wave hello and good morning as they passed my front gate.

Give the negative part of your character a name that identifies it in no more than two words. SELF-TORTURER;

HANGING JUDGE; HI MUM. Say hello in a polite manner every time he, she or it appears. At first the toxic feeling will decrease or vanish for an instant. Repeat your greeting when the negativity reappears. Slowly and over time, the negativity will decrease in intensity and appear less often.

If you are alone, greet your torturer out loud. If you are with people who would think you are mad, do it silently in your head. At first you will not always notice the negativity as a distinct entity. You have been its captive for too long.

This is a slow process. Perseverance is absolutely necessary.

NOTE: *The Ego-Alien Technique* promotes neuroplasticity. Neuroplasticity research shows that the brain, if properly stimulated, can replace entrenched beliefs, can even let healthy parts of the brain take over from damaged parts of the brain. [Read *The Brain That Changes Itself*, by Norman Doidge. An excellent and exciting book.]

Temporal Tapping

TEMPORAL tapping can be used to help eliminate bad habits, toxic beliefs and character traits.

First relax your jaw. Tapping is done with short, sharp, quick, non-painful taps using the soft part of two fingertips.

Taps start at the front centre of the ear, move on to the corner of the eye, and then in a high arch moving upward and slanting over to the top of the ear, ending at the upper outer edge of the ear.

Use positive language and the left hand on the left side of the head. For example, procrastination is going out of my life.

Use negative language and your right hand on the right side of the head. For example, no more will I procrastinate.

[When temporal tapping another person, facing them, reverse the hand you use but keep the left side of their head with positive statements and the right side with "negative" statements as you speak your healing phrases.]

You will feel the statement penetrate surprisingly deep into your consciousness.

Repeat six to eight times daily.

Make your healing statement out loud at first, but it will work from thought or reading the healing statement.

Up to six weeks of effort is usually needed for a distinct result.

I gratefully learned about temporal tapping from Dr. George Goodheart of Detroit.

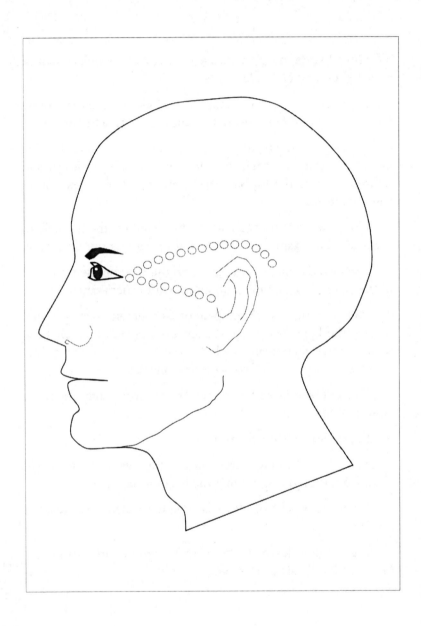

Harvey R. Wasserman

Self-Hypnosis To Intensify Temporal Tapping

A SIMPLE self-hypnotic technique performed just before temporal tapping can significantly intensify the neuroplastic effect of temporal tapping.

Close your eyes and roll them up as if you are trying to look up at the top of your head. Hold your eyes in this position as you slowly count backward from sixty to zero.

Do this out loud if comfortable or silently in your head. Do not rush the count. One number per second is about right.

At zero return your eyes to their normal position and, with your eyes closed, proceed with the temporal tapping. Your self-healing statements will feel as if they had penetrated more profoundly into your mind.

CHAPTER NINETEEN

DEATH AND FEAR

Medical Infallibility
Am I Dead?
The Eleven-Storey Statement

Medical Infallibility

MOST PHYSICIANS are well trained and well intentioned and yet...!

ONE: In my sophomore year at medical school, we were practising electrocardiograms under the junior professor's supervision.

I was the last one to have my electrocardiogram taken. They wired me up and turned on the machine. Everyone gasped in horror, including the professor. He announced in all solemnity that I had inverted T waves, a certain indicator of a fatal cardiac diagnosis. I was feeling fine until my death sentence. In addition, the professor measured my tracing and announced that I had delayed electrical conduction time, a serious confirming finding. He suggested I see a private cardiologist in town.

"Oh my God! No appointments available for two weeks."

All my medical classmates who wore size 42 asked to inherit my clothing after my demise.

I read every book I could find. They confirmed inverted T waves was curtains. I still felt fine.

I read up on measuring cardiac electric transit time. I measured my level at least ten thousand times. I measured and measured it, always normal, but what did I, a lowly second-year medical student, know compared to an assistant professor of medicine?

Finally the consultation. There is one normal heart presentation that throws out the usually deadly T waves and is of no consequence. That finding is a horizontal positioning of the heart in the chest. I had one. The specialist confirmed that my reading of the transit time was absolutely correct. It was normal.

Harvey R. Wasserman

TWO: Interns get x-rays every few months. Stress, over-work, exposure to disease can produce tuberculosis. In the fourth month of my internship, an emergency call from radiology announced a large lung tumour found in my routine x-ray that was most likely malignant.

Repeat emergency chest x-ray was ordered. I was working in the emergency room and asked the head nurse to immediately let me know when radiology called with their results on the second x-ray.

I worked saving lives for three hours, nothing. My head was filled with plans for my exit from this world. When I could stand it no longer, I asked the head nurse if there was a call from radiology.

"Oh yes, I forgot to tell you. The first x-ray film was defective. The film was sick, you're fine".

THREE: When I was fifty-five years old, I had a mild heart attack. I went to a holistic medical clinic for chelation therapy, a new and disputed treatment for arteriosclerotic arteries. A complete medical work-up was required. The head nurse announced I had severe diabetes. What I had was a severe case of misfiled medical reports. At the end of my treatment and work-up, the great head doctor finally sees you for his summary. "All is well" he said. "But my medical assistant has found an enlarged, rock hard prostate." Prostate cancer.

"Would you please re-check my prostate".

"I trust my assistants completely."

It was Saturday; I couldn't get a urological check until Monday.

In a final expression of voice tone (but with civilised content), I threatened to assassinate his highness if he didn't give me a rectal exam.

I didn't not have a rock hard prostate. In fact, it was a bit soft. He exuded some fluid from my penis. Under microscopy, he told me I had a venereal disease, chlamydia. A subsequent trip to a VD specialist established my venereal innocence.

Despite pressure, I cancelled my last cheque. I refused to pay.

FOUR: As an intern, I was sick for a few days with the flu. The training haematologist on the staff took my blood sample.

I was informed that I had abnormal white cells, i.e., leukaemia. Five days later the professor returned and announced that I had normal cells for someone recovering from the flu.

FIVE: Recently I developed an inability to lift my right ankle, "foot drop." The treatment recommended was major spinal surgery. I learned of an advanced Russian device called the Scenar that was developed for self-treatment of astronauts in space. Six weeks later, my ankle was normal!

Am I Dead?

A FIERY SWORD thrust deep into the left side of my neck. Heart attack! I am only 55, rushed to the hospital – cardiac emergency unit.

The unit is designed by a heartless architect for the convenience of the medical staff. Two concentric circles. Outer circle patient beds separated by curtains. Inner circle the nursing station. All is tile white, no windows, no plants or pictures. We are wired at each bed to a monitor suspended from the ceiling. During the night people drop dead while doctors energetically fail to revive them.

At 2 am my monitor goes flat line and howls. My heart has stopped. I am dead. I don't feel dead, but what do I know? I have never been dead before. Ten minutes to discover the monitor is dead.

There is nothing to read. Toilet in bed. To relieve my boredom I somehow learn to control my pulse rate. I make it go up or down at will to entertain the nurses.

After five days I move to a private room. I am to have an angiogram, a picture of the coronary arteries. My chances of dying during the procedure are 0.7%. I call every medical authority I know, no joy; there is no other way to discover the extent of my heart damage.

The night before a junior doctor explains every detail. I am in total terror. My wife is forced to leave after visiting hours. Alone in my terror.

Beams of light in my room. Four of them floating over me, hands reaching into my chest and heart. In thought I ask them to heal any damage. They reply politely, no. My terror is gone, and I sleep.

5 am, I am taken to the cardioscopy room, slightly sedated, only slightly tense. Under an x-ray screen a thin tube is

inserted in a large artery near my groin, run up to my heart and placed in turn in each of the heart's arteries.

Dye for visualisation is inserted in each artery, one at a time. The dye goes through your heart and gives you an undesirable toxic, miserable sensation so bad you wouldn't want to live. It only lasts for thirty seconds.

After each injection you need to cough to drive the blood back into your heart and the dye out so that your heart won't stop.

My consultant shouts in glee, "Look at the screen. You can actually see your coronary arteries. Isn't scientific medicine wonderful!" I look. Fuck this looking shit. I don't want to see my coronary arteries. I want this nightmare to end.

Back in the room, my legs and pelvis are covered with sand bags so the insertion point of the thin tube can clot properly. For fourteen hours you can't move. The aching in my muscles is unbelievable.

It's over. I am alive and back in my room. A window. Every drop of rain a diamond. A falling leaf is pure joy. A bird flying by is a living miracle.

My heart problem is not serious. For two weeks the joy of living, the amazing miracle of the natural world persists and then slowly fades away. I am back to normal. Damn it.

Harvey R. Wasserman

The Eleven-Storey Statement

AT 55 I HAD A HEART ATTACK. The fear didn't leave me. How the hell was I to get over it?

Run a wild river? The Chilco, class five rapids. Mountains stop radio contact. (So wild, too many people drowned. The river now permanently closed for rafters.) Great fun and excitement. It only helped a little.

Hike a mountain ridge in British Columbia. Two and a half feet wide, two thousand foot drop on each side. No way to call for a doctor. Daring, great views. It only helped a little.

Hang gliding – dangerous! I love flying light planes and gliders. Maybe this will do it. The best place in the world, Kitty Hawk Kites in North Carolina. The best and safest in the world. Sand dunes, predictable winds (also attracted the Wright Brothers).

On signing in for five days training, a release of responsibility form so gory that I almost quit then and there.

I will give the first day a try. Suspended by a body protection suit under the wing. Lots of students. I try to be second to launch and learn from the first (no long wait to scare myself).

The hill is small and short. The instructor runs alongside to shout instructions. No way to get hurt.

After the second day, twenty of us are selected to join Mike on the two-storey hill. You can get hurt, but not killed.

First launch, a classic mistake. I counter a crosswind on launch with my shoulder and not my hips. I spin down head first, crash, breaking the wing, bruise my leg and land upside down on top of the hang glider wing.

The instructor has a spare part (it must happen often). I fly again immediately, before I have time to terrify myself. Perfect launch and landing.

After two days of flying, eight of us are chosen to go with Joe – the advanced beginners' class.

An eleven-storey hill. You can get killed.

Instructor. "I know it looks more dangerous, but you have more altitude to correct mistakes."

Me, in thought, *Yes. If you don't correct your mistake, you get killed.* Terror. I hang back last, not second, to launch. *I can quit, no shame.*

Launching is an act of faith and commitment.

Faith – you're holding the wing above you out of sight connected to it by a triangular piece of aluminium tubing.

Commitment – if you don't run like hell and jump, there is no wing lift and you will die.

(I WOULD RATHER DIE HERE TODAY THAN OLD AND SICK AND IN A HOSPITAL.)

I am launched, fifty percent hysterically disassociated (not there).

The wing is designed only to go slowly downhill for a 450 meter flight. Near the ground, you push the aluminium triangle forward, the wing becomes a parachute and you land like a leaf on your feet.

I land on my stomach; everyone else lands on their feet.

Climbing back up the hill is exhausting. The wing weighs sixty-five pounds, and half your steps slide backwards in the sand. I am 58. The other seven are 18 to 25.

The next four launches are an exact duplication of the first.

Launch five. *(I HAVEN'T GOTTEN KILLED. MAYBE I WON'T.)*

On my fifth launch, no terror. I am fully conscious and notice a small hill near the landing site blocking the wind, decreasing wind lift. I turn the wing into a parachute earlier than before. I land on my feet to the raucous cheers of my colleagues.

My fear of a heart attack was gone permanently. For six months all sizes and shapes of fear were gone. Many slowly to return.

Acceptance of death is a major key to living without fear.

CHAPTER TWENTY
MUSIC

Music
Lullaby For Willie

Music

MY UNCLE AL loved to play the violin. He lived with us during the Great Depression until he could support himself.

Inspired by my Uncle Al, I wanted to play the violin. To save money I was sent to the Community Centre in the Jewish slum. I must have been pretty good. I was soon given a scholarship funded by the wife of the US Secretary of the Treasury and loaned a good violin. The scholarship was to provide me with a private Juilliard School music teacher.

I joined the Public School 70 Orchestra, a championship New York City public school orchestra. I was placed in the second violin section. This section plays only the harmony. I loved the first violin melodies and played them instead by ear.

The conductor didn't punish me. After a few weeks, he transferred me to the back of the first violin section. One week later I was made Assistant Concert Master. First violinist Irma Schiff was better than I was. I silently fell in love with her. I could read music, write compositions and play anything I heard.

I stopped playing at thirteen. Later I thought it was in rebellion against my mother. Actually she didn't care. She wanted to produce a doctor. I gave what had become my own un-played violin to a surgeon friend when I started to practice psychiatry.

Thirty-five years later I retired for one year, repossessed my old violin, started to play and took one or two lessons. I was terrible. I couldn't stand the sounds I made and struggled to read music.

I went to a hypnotherapist, hoping to bring back my old skills (to no avail). Regressed to that age I said, "I can't go on. If I do, the sensuality will destroy me." I interpreted that to mean I quit the violin because, to continue, I would have to put all my passion into it, and that passion had to go into academics and medical school.

During the years after I stopped playing, I stopped listening to music. Neither popular nor classical music pleased me. I only listened to African drumbeats and began to master the African talking drums.

After an amazing summer in the wilds of New Guinea, followed by two sensual weeks at the Esalen Institute for Psychotherapy, I flew to New York City on a 747. Lying down over three seats, I plugged in the earphones, and classical music flowed through me, affecting every cell in my body.

I was transfixed. I knew instantly that music can affect every part of the body. You listen with your body and not just your ears. Studying ayurvedic music (an ancient Hindu healing discipline) reinforced this belief.

Aside from my personal enjoyment of music, I use it with my patients. I use ayurvedic music to manipulate consciousness and to reinforce the effect of techniques I have developed.

Dr. Hans Jenny, a Swiss physician who did research in the 1960s, turned sound and music into two and three dimensional configurations using small particles suspended in oil over a loudspeaker. His work shows that sound is not just sound. Each note creates a specific pattern, and some combinations of sound produce three-dimensional figures that seem to move as if they are alive.

No wonder music has played such an important part in human life since the beginning of time.

Lullaby For Willie

SHYAM BHATNAGAR is a Master of one part of Ayurvedic Medicine. Ayurvedic Medicine is the ancient traditional Indian art of healing. Shyam's expertise is the use of sound and music for healing — emotional, spiritual and physical. He can do amazing things with sound. He can diagnose what is wrong with you by listening to your voice. He can direct sound to any part of your body and compose music to promote healing. Shyam is the only one with his training and skills that I have heard of working in the West.

I took some training and treatment with Shyam. At the end of the month of May, he travels to Europe where he teaches in Luxembourg. As he finished my last session before he left, he handed me an audio cassette with the instructions, "Listen to it every night before you go to bed."

I listened that night. I cannot exaggerate the exciting affect the music had on me. It was more exciting than any experience I had known. WOW! I sure was going to listen every night.

After ten nights, my wife complained that there was something wrong with me sexually. Of course I denied it. Twenty nights later I was completely impotent. Never happened to me before!

What could it be? Something I ate? Some deep psychological problem suddenly coming to the fore? The next day I wondered if there was anything new in my life that could totally inhibit my ability to have an erection.

Thought; thought; thought; and then, "THE TAPE." I stopped listening to the tape. Five nights later I was sexually normal. I never listened again. Accidentally on purpose I managed to lose the tape.

Shyam returned in the fall for his next scheduled appointment with me.

"Shyam, your tape made me impotent."

"Didn't I tell you?"

"You didn't tell me a damn thing."

"As I evaluated your personality, I saw you looking into the outside world for excitement, such as living with cannibals, running dangerous rivers, paragliding, etc. I wanted to show you that the most exciting journey is the inner journey. So I wrote for you a piece of music that would give you such an experience, and I did that by writing a melody that would move energy from the lower to the upper chakras. Temporarily, that could cause you impotence."

CHAPTER TWENTY-ONE
HEALING WILDERNESS

Healing Wilderness

Healing Wilderness

I HAVE ALWAYS found travelling in wilderness very rejuvenating. My worries, anxieties, are replaced by peace and happiness.

That mountain in front of me was there long before me and will be there long after me. I am a small part of something large and eternal, and that is ok.

In the 1960s I travelled down the Colorado River through the Grand Canyon on a raft trip. Accompanying us was a very diverse group of people, including a military captain who exalted in killing "gooks" (Vietnamese rebels) and a sweet benevolent nurse. The rest were a bunch of boring conventional people. How could I survive two weeks of intimate living in such a group?

The grandeur of the Canyon, the beauty of the wildflowers and wild cacti began a transformation. The pelting rain, the sand storms, a broken motor that required all our cooperation to navigate the rapids changed everybody. Many of the phenomena of group psychotherapy — warmth, honesty, helpfulness and free, clear communication — occurred spontaneously.

This gave me the idea of doing group psychotherapy while travelling the Colorado River through the Grand Canyon. Wilderness and therapy should intensify each other. I managed to convince ten tenderfeet to come with me. It worked. We achieved a lovely open companionship, even shared a spiritual experience, feeling connected with the universe.

This happened before travel through the Grand Canyon became popular. For two weeks we were the population of our world. We met with no other human beings.

I believe I created wilderness group therapy. It is mentioned in the book , *Please Touch, a Guided Tour of the Human Potential Movement*, by Jane Howard; 1970.

Harvey R. Wasserman

On a subsequent therapy wilderness trip through the Grand Canyon, Betty Fuller, a well-known therapist from California, was swept over a ten foot waterfall of a Colorado tributary, Havasu Creek. Havasu Creek is one of the world's most beautiful rivers, surrounded by wildflowers and wild cactus. Its crystal clear aquamarine waters flow in a series of falls into the Colorado River, where it weaves a great swirling design of aquamarine within the brown of the muddy Colorado.

I was with Betty Fuller when she was swept over one of the falls of the Havasu Creek. She fell over upside down and backwards. She didn't surface immediately. I had to decide whether I could save her without sacrificing myself. I couldn't see her under the water. At the foot of the falls, the mixture of water and air obscured my vision.

I was about to throw myself into the water when Betty emerged, thrusting a sneaker in the air.

"I know what Fritz Perls meant by The Now!" she shouted in triumph.

She had stayed under the water to recover the sneaker she had borrowed from Virginia Satir, which had come off in her plunge over the falls.

In the midst of this overwhelming, possibly dire experience, Betty felt no fear. Living in the moment, there is no fear. Fear is the consequence of imagining future impending disaster.

CHAPTER TWENTY-TWO

DANGEROUS, STUPID THINGS

Dangerous, Stupid Things

Dangerous, Stupid Things

LIONS ARE NOT AFRAID of you if you are inside a car. Stick your head out of the car window, their backs arch. Stay there and they will attack.

Ngorongoro Crater is a vast area in Tanzania filled with wildlife. I was driving my wife, one of my sons and his friend, unaccompanied by a guide.

In the morning we passed a huge solo male lion with a magnificent mane, eating a Thomson gazelle (a small antelope). We watched him munch away for fifteen or twenty minutes, then left and had a glorious day observing almost every wild creature known to central Africa.

On our way back to our lodge we passed him again. He was sleeping. All that was left of the gazelle was a few bones and the top of its skull, displaying a beautiful pair of black antlers. I wanted them.

Without a moment's hesitation or fear, I quietly opened the car door, walked up to the sleeping lion, picked up my souvenir. Walked back to the car and carefully closed the door.

My wife's eyes were wide with terror. "I was terrified."

"Why didn't you say something?"

"I was afraid I would wake up the lion."

When I go on an adventure, I know all the dangers and protect myself by having a companion who is experienced in handling them. But every once in a while I impulsively do something incredibly dangerous with no fear. It's only when I return to safety that I think, "That was a stupid thing to do."

A RHINOCEROS has a sharp, long horn on its nose. A Volkswagen mini bus has a thin sheet of metal on its nose.

The rhino confronted me in my Volkswagen in Ngorongoro Crater. I charged him and stopped. What fun if he charged back and punched a hole in the Volkswagen!

He charged back and stopped short. I charged him again and stopped short. He returned the favour but also stopped short. A third time the same thing happened.

Only then did I realise what a stupid game I was playing. The rhino was wiser than I was.

I have to admit that I was pissed off at the man who rented me the Volkswagen. If I returned it with a hole in the front, how could I be blamed? Probably the damage would be covered by insurance as an Act of God.

I HAVE ALWAYS WANTED to see a volcano erupt, to be close to the power and energy of mother nature displaying her fury from the centre of our earth.

Mauna Loa in Maui, Hawaii, is a vigorous active volcano, the largest in the world. You can walk across its caldera of steaming rock, wondering if an eruption is imminent, until you come to Halemaumau, the open fire pit, a lake of bubbly molten rock.

In Hawaiian legend Pele, the Goddess of Volcanoes, will erupt if you throw a bottle of gin into Halemaumau. What a temptation! Controlled by a wooden fence and an occasional guard, you are not supposed to get close to the fire pit.

Maybe Pele would settle for an orchid. Wild orchids grow in the caldera. I had no gin, so I picked an orchid and making certain no guards were around, crawled under the fence. I kept myself very flat as I crawled to the edge. There I felt the intense heat and discovered the edge was undercut and very thin. I threw in my orchid and made a hasty flat retreat. If I had broken the crust, the lava wouldn't have killed me. I would have been burned to a crisp half way down to the bubbling molten rock.

HAVE YOU EVER LOOKED straight down the flowing edge of a major waterfall? Neither had I. Today I was going to change that.

Virginia Falls, on the Nahanai River in a remote area of the Yukon, is three hundred and sixteen feet high, twice as high as Niagara Falls. You land by sea plane at the top of the falls and transport all your equipment to the bottom of the falls for the trip down the Nahanai River.

The edge of the falls carries only a quarter to a half inch of water and luxurious, verdant slippery algae. I walked slowly and carefully to the edge of the falls. As I admired the power of this World Heritage Site, I suddenly realised I was in great danger. If I slipped over, I would never survive. I sat down and crawled backwards, slowly, carefully, with six points of contact — buttocks, legs and hands — and made it to shore with some terrifying slippage. If I had slipped over, no one would ever have known what happened. I would simply have disappeared. I never told anyone what a stupid thing I had done.

Maybe there is a guardian angel for impulsive fools.

Harvey R. Wasserman

CHAPTER TWENTY-THREE

BIRDS

The Birds Number One
The Birds Number Two
The Birds Number Three
The Birds Number Four

The Birds Number One

THE GARDEN of Eden should be another name for the Galapagos Islands.

They are six hundred miles west of Ecuador, made famous as the place where Charles Darwin added to his theory of evolution. To me they are famous because the creatures that live there are not afraid of man.

Bingo! An idea! Water is scarce.

I glued a paper cup to my hat and filled it with water. Then I sat on a rock near some bushes.

After about ten minutes finches landed on my head (hat), hopped around and drank from my cup.

What magic, what a miracle. Like living in a different world, a world without fear. How utterly delightful.

Harvey R. Wasserman

The Birds Number Two

I WAS SITTING on a ledge in the Galapagos watching a young sea lion give birth. She lay on her side, the baby and the afterbirth came out covered with mucus and blood.

Ten minutes later, oh my God! A hawk landed six inches to my right. Then another hawk and more hawks perched next to me, four on each side.

They totally ignored me. They were staring intently at the mother and child and afterbirth. I sat very still.

The hawks launched an attack for the afterbirth. Mama counterattacked and got a few tail feathers before they escaped.

The attack and defence continued for about fifteen minutes. During a brief pause, Mama licked the blood and mucus off her baby and let the hawks take their prize.

She seemed at last to be able to tell the difference between the baby and the afterbirth.

The Birds Number Three

NAMIBIA HAS so many wild animals that they serve wildebeest, alligator and many varieties of antelopes in restaurants.

While camping in a remote wilderness area, quietly eating a breakfast sandwich , three black birds the size of Jackdaws landed on my hat. I have a picture to prove it.

They jumped around for a while. I sat very still. Two of them got into a fight, fell to the ground, fought it out, made up and flew back to my hat.

No one had ever seen this happen before.

The next day, at a different remote site, I put crumbs on my hat. Nothing happened.

The Birds Number Four

AN ORNITHOLOGIST was studying native birds in a remote area of the Jimmy Valley of New Guinea.

Some birds were captured and kept in cages. Some wild birds felt safe. A very large bird landed on my head.

Then, a miracle! A large wild hornbill sat on my lap, my thumb in its giant beak.

Notice my delight.

Index of Exercises

Photos and Credits

Cover Painting, *Viva Mexico!*, acrylic on canvas, 16" x 40", Harvey R Wasserman, 2008

Cover concept, Sarah Daniel

Photos, page 8   Harvey as 'Big John', Papua New Guinea, 1971

Photo, page 294   Harvey and birds, Namibia, 2008

Photo, page 295   Harvey and hornbill, Papua New Guinea, 1971

Photo, page 296   Harvey with bird on head, Papua New Guinea, 1971

Co-editing, Sarah Daniel

Image Design, Ben Geoghegan
[http://bengeoghegan.blogspot.com/]

Harvey's Website: http://harveywasserman.ie

Lightning Source UK Ltd.
Milton Keynes UK
KOW04f2135201014